Let Christ Transform Your Pain:

How Jesus Can Use Your Suffering to Bring About a Greater Good

by Dr. Elizabeth Stewart

For Colin, Tanya and Jessica

"May we all glorify You and give proof of our love for You by bearing courageously and even joyously the cross which is ours."

From the Daily Offering Prayer for members of the Catholic Union of the Sick in America

Preface

Why another book on suffering? There are already so many, and sometimes it seems as though everything that can be said on this subject has already been written.

My perspective is a little different from most, however.

I live with suffering every day, and I know what it feels like. I've learned how to accept it, and how to turn it to good use – at least, most of the time, which is all we can ask of ourselves.

Suffering is – for the most part – completely unsought.

We don't ask for it, we don't want it, and most of us would like nothing more than for our pain to disappear.

Whether we are suffering from mental, physical or spiritual pain, we'd like to be free from it. We have pain-killers for every type of physical pain, and there is no shame in taking them. But when faced with emotional or spiritual suffering, it's much harder to find relief. What seem like balms for the soul can be dangerous – drugs are addictive, but so are harmful relationships for many of us, and gambling, food and alcohol too often lead to even worse states, possibly to premature death.

Yet, I believe that we can look at suffering differently.

What if suffering proved to be a blessing, not a curse?

What if suffering were actually a gift from God?

What if, through accepting our pain, we were able to offer Him something uniquely valuable, which only we can give Him?

And suppose that – as we can see in the lives of others – we could see suffering as a doorway to greater life?

We might find that what we thought was a terrible burden turns out to be our own personal way towards the path of Union with God. We are all called to be saints, and perhaps it is through our own suffering, our own particular cross, that we will ultimately know the joy and bliss of living each day ever closer to the Father, in the company of all the saints both known and unknown who have trodden this way before us.

Suffering may turn out to be the hidden jewel God has placed in our lives so that we might attain this great joy, and finally live in eternity with Him.

If you are reading this book, it is not by chance. You may be suffering yourself, or perhaps you are close to someone whose pain seems unbearable, and you cannot see any possible benefit. Perhaps you are hoping to find some light at the end of a particular tunnel. Or perhaps you are simply curious.

Whatever you wish for, I hope you will find it, and if my book helps you even a little as you struggle to accept a difficult situation, I will be very glad.

Here, then, is my own humble offering to those in pain, with my prayers that you might find some relief.

*   *   *

Many have written about suffering, but among them there are relatively few whose authors have the particular set of qualifications that I possess, thanks to a near-catastrophic car crash more than 30 years ago.

That crash – which smashed all my bones from my pelvis to my ankles, punctured my lung, ruptured my bladder and tore my nerves literally to shreds – has left me in constant pain. I need a wheelchair to get around. I depend on the loving care of my husband to allow me to live as normally as possible; without him, I would not be able to live at home.

Severe pain is a daily companion, alleviated to some extent

by my painkillers, but always waiting in the wings.

Mentally, the crash made me aware of two things: I'm an alcoholic and have bi-polar disease. These two illnesses were the indirect cause of my crash. I have to live with these companions, too. Their voices speak to me each day, and I've learned to listen, thank them for sharing, and then carry on with my life.

But the crash also brought me the greatest blessings which could have reached me in no other way. For these, I thank God each day.

First, He gave me two very vivid and unforgettable Near Death Experiences, the first as firemen cut through the metal of my car to lift my broken body on to a stretcher. The second followed a few days later, during the first of two 16-hour operations undertaken by a team of top orthopaedic surgeons, who together saved my life and helped to turn it completely around.

The first experience was the longer of the two, and brought me through the dark tunnel that others have written about, into the very bright light of a new dimension. I don't know whether that was Heaven or Purgatory; it was somewhere beyond death, and quite, quite different from anywhere on Earth.

The light emanated from a tall, beautiful, loving Person who received me into His arms and held me as I struggled to find my bearings. I knew this Person was Jesus Christ and that He loved me beyond all imagining. I was in a state of bliss as He held me close, and wanted nothing more than to be in this great Presence for ever.

But it was not to be.

As I slowly began to adjust to the light, Jesus showed me a mental picture – my two children, aged six and ten.
And He silently told me that I had to make a choice.

I could remain in this place of great happiness, enjoying the knowledge that I was on my way to Heaven and to the Eternal Presence of God. So strong was this urge that I desired nothing more in that moment.

Or I could return to Earth, to be with my children.

Of course, I chose to return. They were so dear, so beloved, so very precious that the thought of being without them was terrible. My marriage to their father had broken up, and without me they would have no parent living with them. It was no contest.

As soon as I had chosen, the vision of Jesus began to recede and I travelled through the dark tunnel once more, back to life.

A life that would never be the same.

The second Near Death Experience was very similar to the first, except it seemed to last for a shorter time because my choice was already made. I saw the team of surgeons operating on me, witnessed their battle, and cheered them on in silence from a space about twenty feet above the operating table.

I was in hospital for almost four months.

Nobody thought I would survive the accident. The doctors told me they had at first believed I would die from internal bleeding. I had lost so much blood that I had to be given twelve pints in a transfusion, when the body normally carries only nine! But against all the odds I pulled through and came round in the Intensive Care ward.

The second great obstacle was learning to move and even to walk a little. This was another milestone that doctors thought impossible, but in the years that followed the accident I did manage to walk, though always with the support of a stick or similar aid.

Alas, the nature of my injuries meant that every day my bones and muscles were deteriorating, and today, as I mentioned, I use a wheelchair to get around. Although so many of my joints were replaced, there is still pain from arthritis and from old wounds that had not completely healed. One unhealed fracture in my leg causes extreme pain when I put any weight on it, and I've been told I have so little bone left that no more replacement surgery will be possible. The pain I have today will only increase with time.

The neuropathic pains are the most difficult to deal with. My nerves did eventually grow back, but in the wrong way. Instead of telling my muscles to move, they simply magnify what would normally be a minor ache into a difficult bout of sciatica that can last for hours, even days.

I can't tell where my left leg is unless I look at it. I can't make the muscles move on that side, and in my feet I have points that are numb and points that are horribly sensitive.

To top it all, thanks to my enforced immobility I now have Type 2 diabetes, and must carefully monitor everything I eat.

And yet, I'm truly grateful for everything that happened to me.

Why?

Because God used all my suffering to bring me closer to Him.

That was the second great gift He gave me, after the Near Death Experiences; the knowledge, the absolute certainty, that this loving presence – Jesus Christ – is always there, always ready to comfort me and to show me how good may be brought forth from what would otherwise be a dreadful waste of pain.

In hospital, I began to read the Autobiography of St Therese of Lisieux, and it was she who first showed me the way that pain can be transmuted into joy.

I have written at length about my accident, my recovery, and my conversion to the Catholic faith in my first book, "*A Raging Thirst*".

In this book, however, I want to pass on the truths I learned from my own suffering, truths I could discover in no other way.

It's my profound desire that you may come to know the peace and joy that I have been given, no matter what your suffering may involve or what form it takes.

God is always there, just waiting for us to turn to Him so that He can heal and bless and comfort us. And you can prove this for yourself, as I will show you in this book.

Introduction

Suffering is the guest that nobody wants.

Uninvited, it erupts into your life and steals your joy and peace.

With no departure date, you fear that suffering may never leave. And yet, you cannot rid yourself of it by willpower; you can't simply wish it away.

"Why me?" many cry out – why must it happen to me? What did I do to deserve this?

"Well, why *not* you?" your rational self may reply. "Everyone has their share of pain and grief, so why should you alone escape?"

Interestingly, we never ask this question of equally undeserved happiness and joy. We accept them as our due, and never ask why they have come to us.

With suffering, however, we try to reason it away, and yet, reason alone doesn't help.

A story is told of a young woman, recently widowed and inconsolable in her mourning, who went to a renowned sage to ask his advice.

"What can I do to rid myself of this pain?" she asked him. "Tell me, and I'll do anything you say. I can't bear to live with this burden for the rest of my life."

"It is hard," the sage agreed, "but there is something you can do to help yourself. You must visit every house in your village and seek a home that has never experienced any sadness. When you have done this, come back to me."

The young widow did as the sage bade her, and searched for days to find a single home that had never known grief. Of course, her search was fruitless.

Disappointed at her failure, she returned to the sage and berated him.

"Why did you tell me to do this? I have failed. I have found no one, not one single person, who has never known suffering."

The sage looked at her with compassion.

"You see now that suffering is common to all people. This knowledge will open your heart and lead you to peace."

After many more years, the widow, now old and wise, became known for her calm acceptance of pain. People sought her out when they had troubles, finding in her loving presence a balm for their souls. Her own grief dissolved in the ocean of pain that she now saw was the human lot, and she realized that relief lies first of all in acceptance, and then in helping others carry their own burdens.

This story has spread around the world, told variously of Buddhist, Hindu, Jewish and Muslim sages. And there is indeed much truth and solace in it; for our ability to look beyond our own pain and, with compassion and understanding, to attempt to heal the sorrows of others, is one of the fruits of suffering.

There is a huge difference, however, between the Catholic attitude to suffering and that of other religions and belief systems.

Suffering in the Buddhist and Hindu faiths is part of one's karma, your problems arising from misdeeds in past lives. In this view, if we have injured someone's legs in a previous life, we may break our own bones in this life. The only remedy is to live stoically with our pain and hope for better karma next time around.

To a Christian, the prospect of an endless cycle of lives fraught with pain and disease, going on and on with no relief in sight, is disturbing, to say the least. Both Buddhists and Hindus believe that living as compassionately as possible cuts the risk of suffering in future lives, but there is no certainty about this.

Neither Hindus nor Buddhists offer any clear vision of God or of a future with Him in Paradise, as we Christians believe. Hinduism has many gods and goddesses, any of which may inflict injury or confer benefits at will. Trying to please them all is impossible.

And if, as Hindus say, our suffering is because of our karma, there is no compulsion or moral impulse for anyone to relieve the sufferings of another. We may do more harm than good in this view; taking away someone's pain could mean they only meet it again in their next incarnation, which may not even be as a human being. We might come back as a cockroach, to be stepped on, if we have not expiated our sins and purified our karma.

No wonder Mother Teresa of Calcutta made such a deep impression on the Indian public. For the first time, through the media, Hindus saw one saintly woman working round the clock, relieving the suffering of dying people. That one woman would do this amazed them, but even more incredible, to the Hindu, was the attraction that such a person exercised. Her lone efforts are now multiplied across continents with an order that recruits Christian women to relieve the suffering that others pass by.

Buddhists do offer compassionate help to those in need, but the supreme spiritual achievement of this faith is to free oneself of all attachments so that, eventually, one will die without needing to return to Earth. Their word "Nirvana" does not refer to our "Heaven", for nirvana is a state of universal consciousness in which the individual soul is extinguished. To live in a state of complete emotional detachment, with the prospect of final extinction, is not a doctrine that Christians can embrace. It is quite contrary to the teachings of Christ.

The Jewish faith comes closest to our own concept of suffering, as we might expect. To Jews, suffering exists so that we may grow in love and compassion by helping those less fortunate than ourselves. The chief duty of a Jewish doctor is to save life, and to take away pain. Suffering does not have any intrinsic value in Judaism, but exercising loving kindness, especially to those who cannot make us any return, brings us closer to God, our Father in Heaven.

Islam offers little hope to those who suffer, the Koran merely stating that "Verily we have created man into toil and struggle". True, this religion enjoins charity towards the poor, but most interpret this as towards other Muslims and not "infidels", those who belong to other faiths.

The Sufis, the mystics of Islam, developed a teaching that in many ways echoes Christianity, and encourages its followers to suffer willingly. Nevertheless, the beneficial effects of such sufferings are mostly concerned with elevating the Sufi's own soul, and because they do not accept Christ, they cannot join their own suffering to His.

As for the New Age teachings that blossomed in the second half of the 20th century and have now spread throughout what used to be Christendom, they have nothing at all to teach us about suffering.

Basically, New Age beliefs are very similar to those of Hindus and Buddhists, from which most of them are derived. By way of Theosophy, most New Agers now look on pain and suffering as being the fault of the sufferer. He or she has attracted their afflictions by their own past actions or even by the "wrong" state of mind.

By thinking differently, New Agers believe, anyone can change their circumstances. This false belief– which is the doctrine of wishful thinking elevated to a ridiculous height – causes others to blame the victim for their fate. It is a sort of spiritual self-help culture.

I was once told firmly by a well-meaning New Ager that my arthritis was my own fault, because I thought too rigidly! No, I told her, it came from a car accident that shattered my bones and had nothing to do with my present state of mind. No change of thought patterns could take it away.

Somewhat similar is the "Christian prosperity" teachings of certain evangelists. They exhort us to pray better, pray harder, pray longer – because if we are not prospering, if we are suffering from ill health or poverty or any other affliction, we are simply not approaching God in the right way. Again, the victim is blamed for their own pain.

The Catholic faith has a very different approach, however.

Through studying the words of the saints and most especially of Jesus Christ Himself, we learn that what seems like useless suffering can become a tremendous gift if only we use it wisely.

Suffering may be, as in the Leonard Cohen song, "The crack where the light gets in". Cohen took this image from the Jewish Cabbalistic tradition, but that teaching finds its fullest expression in the Catholic and Orthodox Christian faith.

How that can happen is the theme of this book. I shall refer to the Catholic faith, because that is what I know best, but most Catholic teaching on suffering is also to be found in Orthodoxy. Please take them as equivalent when you read this book.

In talking of suffering, there is one important exception; I'm not referring here to the suffering of children or of animals. That is horrible – loathsome - and we must do everything we can to prevent or alleviate it.

The suffering I shall talk about here refers to the ordinary –
and sometimes extraordinary – pain which comes into the lives
of men and women, people like you and me.

I hope you will accompany me in this journey through the
Christian teachings on suffering, learning from the great
wisdom and supernatural insights of our saints and from the
Lord.

Let's start with a look at the life of St. Therese of Lisieux,
the great saint and Doctor of the Church, whose teachings on
suffering changed my life.

Chapter One:

St Therese and her teachings on suffering

In the autumn of 1897, a young French nun lay dying. For the past two years she had battled with tuberculosis, which in those days was nearly always fatal. Her sufferings had been almost beyond endurance; her fragile flesh could take no more. Already it seemed as though the light of eternity was beginning to shine through the frail, bony "envelope", her term for her body.

All around the little French town of Lisieux, in Normandy, the grain harvest was being gathered in, while in the Carmelite convent a different sort of harvest was being prepared: the release of the soul of this unknown young woman for its journey to eternity.

She can hardly have been comforted by the stinging words of one of her fellow Carmelites, who, bringing her some broth, remarked unkindly, "You are certainly not a saint. In fact, you're hardly a good nun."

To her sisters in the convent, the young woman who lay on her deathbed had not, apparently, achieved any great spiritual heights. As far as they knew, she had lived quietly and simply and had not undertaken any special austerities or gleaned any great insights.

This apparent insignificance led to some anxiety among the community as Therese's illness progressed. Clearly, she had not long to live, and at the death of a nun it was the Carmelite custom to circulate an obituary letter outlining the important facts and spiritual achievements of her life.

In Therese's case, this presented a problem.

"What on earth are we going to say about Sister Therese?"
one nun wondered, echoing the thoughts of many in the convent.
"She has done nothing special and we won't have much to write
about her."

How wrong they were!

This young nun was, of course, the great Saint Therese of
Lisieux, and her original and profound teachings were to
transform the lives of millions of men and women throughout
the world.

She is now not only canonized but given the title of Doctor
of the Church, an honour granted to very few.

Many miracles have been attributed to the intervention of
this beloved saint, and her Basilica at Lisieux is a popular
pilgrimage destination. Hundreds of thousands of pilgrims
come every year to honour St Therese and give thanks for her
intercession. Walls of brass plaques testify to the miracles she
has wrought and the gratitude of her followers.

I am one of those whose life was changed when I read her
autobiography.

It was through gratitude to St. Therese that I was inspired to
write this book, and I hope to show how her teachings can help
many others to find spiritual and mental healing in the midst of
difficulties.

It is my dearest wish that through discovering how St.
Therese and other mystics and saints handled pain and distress,
you will find hope when you yourself face the darkness of
suffering.

First, I shall give a brief outline of St. Therese's life, for the
benefit of readers who may not be familiar with her story.

If you already know the basic facts of her biography, you may want to skip the rest of this chapter and go straight to Chapter Two, where I explain in more detail her practice of offering everything to Jesus. In this offering she included all her physical and mental sufferings, and this is where her teaching becomes very practical for everyone undergoing any type of pain.

Of course, the Catholic doctrine of "offering up" everything to the Lord is not original to St Therese, but the clarity with which she explained it, and the methods she used in daily life to put it into practice, were and still are the source of great consolation to millions of men and women all over the world, both Christian and those of other faiths.

*   *   *

Therese Martin was born in Alencon on January 2, 1873, to a middle-class family. She was the youngest of nine children born to Louis and Zelie Martin, of whom only five survived infancy.

The family were materially comfortable. Zelie was a lace-maker who employed a number of piece-workers to create the world-famous Alencon lace, while Louis was a skilled watchmaker. Nevertheless, they lived frugally, giving generously to the poor, and leading devout Catholic lives. Originally, both Louis and Zelie had believed themselves to be called to a Religious life, and when they accepted this was not to be, married with the intention of living chastely, in a so-called "mariage blanc".

Thank goodness a wise confessor pointed out to them that this was not God"s will for the young couple, for if they had continued to live as brother and sister the world would have been deprived of a great saint.

In fact, all five of their surviving daughters became nuns, and both Louis and Zelie were canonized, together, in 2015, a

9

rare example of a saintly married couple.

Therese has told us in her memoirs that her early childhood held many memories of smiles and caresses. Although as a tiny infant she contracted enteritis, the serious illness which had claimed the lives of three of her baby sisters, she made a full recovery, and was sent for a while to live with a wet-nurse on a smallholding outside Alencon.

Back with her family at the age of fifteen months, Therese was a normal, healthy child who was cosseted as the youngest, and who loved her mother fiercely, following her around the house and constantly calling to her for attention as she mastered various childhood tasks such as learning to climb the stairs.

All the more tragic, then, was the early death of Zelie, who died of breast cancer when Therese was only four years old.

The small girl had heard her mother's stifled cries of pain and had seen the coffin carried into the house.

"I knew very well what it was," she later wrote, and she and her father knelt by the bedside while Zelie received the Last Rites.

From then on, Therese's life changed drastically. She wrote later that the death of her mother made her morbidly over-sensitive and diffident, crying if anyone should look at her, and only happy when people ignored her or when she was alone with her family.

Louis Martin was now the only parent of the young family. Fortunately he was sufficiently wealthy to be able to sell his business and move himself and all five daughters to Lisieux, where they had relatives who could help with the children's upbringing. The house where they lived, Les Buissonets, is now part of the St. Therese pilgrimage route.

It was a fairly small house with a large garden, where the

young Therese played happily with her sisters and enjoyed the attentions of her father, who joined her in the garden and took her on fishing trips to the country.

Nevertheless, despite the physical comfort and family affection that surrounded her, Therese's childhood was punctuated with long spells of unhappiness. She missed her mother dreadfully; she was a misfit at the local school, where other girls thought her strange and ostracised her; and when her older sister Pauline entered the Carmelite monastery in Lisieux, Therese was devastated.

The loss precipitated a serious mental illness in Therese, which defied the efforts of the local doctors to treat it. Accompanied at times by painful physical symptoms, the sickness caused her great distress. Although it was eventually diagnosed as mainly "a neurotic attack", possibly what would today be termed a form of prolonged hysteria, the illness seemed to some, including Therese herself, to be at least partly demonic in origin.

It was as though the devil, scenting a future saint who would threaten his power, was trying to defeat her in advance.

Therese sensed the beginning of a cure when she was ten years old, six months after the first signs of the illness.

A statue of the Virgin Mary stood in Therese's bedroom, and as the girl looked at it, it seemed to her that Mary smiled at her. This brought her great joy and peace, but after a while she began to suffer from the spiritual problem of scruples, and even to doubt that she had experienced her vision.

Therese finally overcame her childish over-sensitivity and fears on Christmas Eve, 1886.

In France it was the custom for children to leave their shoes out for "Baby Jesus" to fill with gifts, in the way that "Father Christmas" or "Santa Claus" delivers presents to children around the world.

As usual that night Therese left out her shoes, but as she made her way upstairs to bed she overheard her father say to Celine, her older sister, "Therese is far too old for this now. Fortunately, it will be the last year!"

Celine followed Therese upstairs and, as the latter began to cry at the untypically harsh words from their father, she attempted to console her.

It was then, Therese recalled, that the real miracle took place.

Suddenly, she was freed from the shackles of self-pity and misery. She wiped her eyes, ran downstairs, and "discovered" the shoes, which were now filled with presents. As if nothing had happened, Therese unwrapped the gifts and exclaimed with joy at each one. Nobody would have suspected she had just been deeply hurt by her father's words, so completely had she mastered herself.

Therese later wrote, "In an instant Jesus, content with my good will, accomplished the work I had not been able to do in ten years."

She explained, "On that blessed night, the sweet infant Jesus, scarcely an hour old, filled the darkness of my soul with floods of light. By becoming weak and little, for love of me, He made me strong and brave. He put His weapons into my hands so that I went on from strength to strength, beginning, if I may say so, 'to run as a giant.'"

She had recovered the strength of soul which had deserted her ever since the death of her mother, and this strength was to remain with her for the rest of her life.

Therese was to face more losses, including the entry into Carmel of another older sister, Marie, and the attempts of yet another, Leonie, to find a religious house where she might fulfill her own vocation.

Celine, the sister closest in age to Therese, also eventually entered Carmel, after Therese herself had been admitted, and when their father, Louis, became too weak and confused to live at home any more.

All five of the Martin sisters were called to the cloister, and four of them – Marie, Pauline, Celine and Therese – lived in the same Carmel, that of Lisieux.

Therese had felt her vocation growing in her from the time of her Christmas Eve "conversion," and she became one of the youngest women to enter Carmel, at the age of fifteen, in 1888.

It took courage and determination for her to have done so, for she had to convince local and regional clergy, and at one point took advantage of a trip to the Vatican to appeal to the Holy Father himself. In the end, Therese's vocation was accepted, and her religious life began.

As we saw earlier, Therese's life as a postulant, novice and then novice-mistress was outwardly quite unremarkable, and this was just as she wished. We would have known nothing of her spiritual progress, her struggles and her graces, let alone have received the exceptional teaching of what has been called her Little Way, had it not been for Pauline, known in Carmel as Sister Agnes.

It was she who, after talking about some childhood memories, mentioned to Therese, now Sister Therese of the Child Jesus and of the Holy Face, that it would be interesting if she could write down some of her own recollections about their family life.

The result was the world-famous "Story of a Soul", written in spare moments and during times of great physical weakness as well as in periods of relative good health. Therese herself attached no great importance to it, and neither did anyone else at the time, for Pauline put it away in a drawer and then forgot about it.

So it was that Therese continued to live with her sisters an ordinary, apparently quite unremarkable, life hidden in the desert of Carmel with her sisters and with her Spouse, Jesus. She had wanted to be sent to a distant convent, somewhere far away, where she could live among people who knew little or nothing about Christianity, but her health prevented this.

Although she seemed well enough when she entered the convent, she contracted tuberculosis at a very young age, probably when she nursed a number of nuns who were seriously ill with Spanish flu.

The first sign of her approaching death came in 1896, after she had observed the convent's rigorous Lenten fast.

On the eve of Good Friday Therese went to bed as usual, but felt a strange sensation, which she described as "... something like a bubbling stream mounting to my lips." Not knowing what it might be and refusing to disobey the rule by relighting her lamp, she waited until morning before looking to see what had happened.

Her handkerchief was soaked in blood.

She understood at once what this meant.

Coughing up blood meant tuberculosis, and tuberculosis meant death.

Therese's response was, to modern minds, astonishing.

"Ah! My soul was filled with a great consolation," she wrote. "I was interiorly persuaded that Jesus, on the anniversary of His own death, wanted to have me hear His first call!"

Not many people, even in that more devout age, would have

greeted the evidence of approaching death with such joy, but then Therese was no ordinary person, no ordinary nun, in spite of that insulting declaration by an unkind sister to the effect that Therese had never done anything special.

Therese had, in fact, lived an entirely special life, her devotion and her understanding reaching profound depths while nobody suspected the great transformation which was taking place inside her soul.

She wrote her autobiography in whatever moments she could snatch from the busy life of the convent. Even while extremely ill, Therese asked for no mitigation of the Rule of Life but endeavoured to observe every detail that was asked of a Carmelite nun in those days.

Forced at last by her superiors to rest and – in the summer of 1897 – to accept her enfeebled state, Therese consented to move to the infirmary. She died there, surrounded by her fellow nuns and in the company of her familial sisters, Pauline, Marie and Celine. At the moment of her death she was seen to experience great bliss and joy, which – a witness said – lasted "for the time of a Credo".

Her last words were "My God ... I love Thee!"

Therese had once said that she wanted to "spend her Heaven doing good on Earth", and her wish was realized almost immediately after her death.

In 1898 a small edition of her "Autobiography of a Soul" was published to great acclaim amongst the Carmelite community. Therese's "Little Way", her guide to the spiritual life for ordinary men and women, spread furiously, and soon the Pope was forced to dispense with the rule that the process of canonization must not be started until 50 years after the subject's death.

Only 26 years after her death, Therese was beatified by Pope

Pius XI, and in the year of Jubilee, 1925, he pronounced her a saint.

Two years later she was named as patroness of foreign missions, an honour she now shared with the great St. Francis Xavier, and as we have seen, she was ultimately proclaimed as a Doctor of the Church.

In her autobiography, St. Therese had explained her attitude to suffering. Everything she found difficult, from putting up with the distracting noise of a nun who was clicking her rosary beads, to suffering the agony of her protracted death, she offered to God, uniting it with the sufferings of Christ on the cross.

"I understood that to become a saint one had to suffer much, seek out always the most perfect thing to do, and forget self," she wrote.

By these deceptively simple means, St. Therese attained to the sainthood she so much desired. It is in following her "Little Way", as her complete spiritual teaching became known, that we too may achieve great things, no matter how small or insignificant our offerings to God may appear.

To help all who wish to imitate her method, St Therese began her work on Earth very soon after her entry into heaven. It was only then that her mission would reach its fullness, and she is very active today in the lives of many – including Muslims as well as Christians – as many healings and miracles attest.

Her early years, her formation by her mother and older sisters, and her later life in Carmel, all combined in the making of a great saint, whose teachings have influenced countless souls.

In the next chapter we will look at these early experiences and her later application of the lessons she first learned at home.

Chapter Two

Therese's teachings on the Little Way and on the use of suffering

The practices of devout Catholics in the France of more than a hundred years ago may seem excessive to us. In the post-modern, post-Christian mindset of the West in the 21st century, many have become accustomed to a lukewarm version of the Catholic faith, what might be called "Catholicism Lite". We want the blessings, but we won't make the effort.

To rise at the break of day in order to attend Mass; to give alms to all who asked; to offer constant little sacrifices to Jesus for the good of other souls – all these were part of daily life for many French families in the time of St Therese. They were practices that many other Catholics in different countries also observed, and still do, though in far fewer numbers than during the late 19th century

In their fidelity to the faith, however, the Martin family were noteworthy even in that more pious age. They attended the early morning Mass, which was known as "the Mass of the poor", and gave alms to any beggars they met along the way. In their home and family life, Zelie and Louis Martin believed the best and easiest way of putting into practice their great faith was to offer sacrifices, and they taught this method to their daughters.

We've seen how Therese's early life, before her mother's untimely death, was happy and serene. In this secure home, Zelie Martin and her older daughters taught the young Therese to make her own small sacrifices because it would please Jesus.

To help them in their efforts, the girls all possessed special chaplets with movable beads. The chaplets were in use at a Visitation boarding school where Marie Martin had been a pupil, and the practice was recommended by St Ignatius. Marie brought chaplets home with her and taught her family how to use them.

Whenever a little sacrifice was made – perhaps the refusal of a favourite food with the intention of offering the effort to Jesus, or giving extra alms from their small allowances to a beggar outside the church – a bead would be moved from one side of the chaplet to the other.

"The most charming thing of all is to see Therese slip her hand into her pocket time and time again, and move a bead along as she makes some sacrifice," Marie once wrote to Pauline.

At the end of the day, the number of sacrifices could easily be seen, and a sense of one's spiritual state might be deduced.

Pauline, who took to the practice immediately, once illustrated to Therese the nature of sacrifice with a simple demonstration. She offered Therese a glass of water, and then invited her to refuse to drink it, even though she was thirsty, so that she might offer up this sacrifice to save a sinner. Therese obeyed her sister, but some time later, having noticed that Therese was thirsty, Pauline offered her a second glass. This time, Pauline explained, she was ordering her sister to drink it, and if Therese obeyed once more she would have the merit of obedience, another form of sacrifice to offer to God.

These early examples played a large part in the formation of Therese's attitude later as a Carmelite nun. She already appreciated the need for constant sacrifice, and she knew, as did her sisters, that life in Carmel would be hard and full of physical and mental trials. Yet, because such a life offered such a large opportunity to please God and to save other souls, the suffering it contained was an attraction to all the Martin sisters.

Indeed, when a nun entered Carmel, this was the life she freely chose, and she could expect no mitigation of the rule for sickness. Life in the Carmel of the late nineteenth century was harsh: nuns suffered from the cold, from the lack of sleep, often from inadequate meals. Novices and mature nuns alike were constantly alert to their own faults and ready to accuse themselves and others of not following the Rule. As we shall see, this aspect of Carmelite life was very significant in helping Therese to develop a mature spirituality.

Greater than the particular physical and mental sufferings inherent in the convent life, however, was the voluntary suffering such a life incurred. Ida Gorres describes this form of suffering as "primarily, acceptance of what comes along; it is no more and no less than the necessary measure of grief and tribulation which afflicts the most commonplace of human lives".

Unlike those of us living in the world, Religious have no easy ways of escape from this daily suffering. They can't use television or films, or romantic novels, or alcohol or gambling or sex in order to numb their feelings. All experiences in convent life – its humdrum nature, the monotony of the predictable daily routine, the petty annoyances and irritations caused by other members of the community - must be lived through to the end, without complaint, and that itself can constitute heroic virtue.

Today, we may well feel a certain disquiet in looking at the "cash register" approach to suffering that was so widely taught in Therese's time. Was there not a danger that, after making sacrifices, the individual was exposed to the greatest sin of all, that of Pride? It might lead to the smug, self-righteous attitude of the Pharisee – thinking that, unlike others, I am not a sinner, because I have fasted every day, given alms and made a large number of sacrifices, so God must be pleased with me. Indeed, this could well happen, and to counteract it, Therese and her sisters constantly kept in mind the many times they had failed each day.

If we stay aware of the difference between what we have

managed to do for God, and where we have fallen short, and if we simply accept our failures without giving in to despair, we will gradually achieve a state of inner peace. We will unflinchingly see our own and other people's weaknesses, and realize that we cannot become worthy by our own efforts, that only God can help us in our efforts to grow to maturity in the spiritual life.

Therese saw that when we undergo any form of suffering, we have a choice. We can accept it as part of God's Will for us, or we can regard it as a useless hardship which we would rather not undergo.

When we accept it, we accept God; when we go even further, and join it to Christ's suffering in his Passion, we elevate our personal suffering into a real sacrifice. Such a sacrifice, flowing from love, becomes noble and acceptable to God, acquiring infinite value because it is taken up into Christ's own great suffering. Through it, we are able to help Him in his great work of salvation; it is that important, that significant.

In a letter to her sister Celine, referring the distress both felt in respect of their father's illness, Therese writes "The canticle of suffering united to (Jesus's) sufferings is what delights His heart the most". And further on in the same letter, she adds, "To be the spouse of Jesus we *must* resemble Jesus, and Jesus is all bloody, He is crowned with thorns."

The acceptance of every form of suffering that God deigns to send us is what pleases Him, this Therese knew; yet, because of her early home experience, when she was taught to count up the number of sacrifices she had made, it might have been tempting for the young nun to see herself as full of merit, and having a large "bank account in heaven".

Therese knew that any merit she possessed came from God, and that by herself she could do nothing. She writes in her autobiography that if Jesus had not taken charge of her soul early on in her life, she might have committed great sins. And since Therese was so honest in her writing, we may take this at face value. She must have realized how great was the temptation to pride or to other sins, and she also knew that everything in us that is good, that is virtuous, is given to us by God and is to be used for His glory.

Therese illustrates the last point when she writes that she has no wish at all to hold on to any merit she may have accumulated. She desired that all her sufferings, all her sacrifices, should be freely given to Jesus to be used as He wished. Above all, she prayed that her sufferings might be used to save souls, to quench the thirst of Jesus on the Cross, when He cried out, "I thirst!" Therese interpreted this cry as the longing of the Lord for souls to come to Him and to be saved.

"Jesus wills to make their salvation depend on one sigh from our heart," Therese wrote on another occasion, explaining her wish to save others by her suffering. "If one sigh can save a soul, what can sufferings like ours not do?"

Explaining that the fruits of her suffering were for Jesus alone to use, Therese said, shortly before her death, "I hold nothing in my hands. Everything I have, everything I merit is for the Church and for souls."

Therese's last great trial, undergone at the same time that she was experiencing extreme physical and mental suffering because of her illness, consisted of what St John of the Cross calls the Dark Night of the Soul. It is the suffering that the soul must undergo when she is deprived of all the previous comforts of her faith, when she has to continue to live and to suffer without any heavenly consolation at all.

Therese said that, although she might appear to be enjoying consolations, it was not so. She felt as though she was no longer close to God, and that she was painfully making her way through darkness, underground, without any vision of heaven or sense of being loved by Jesus.

In her stoical acceptance of this terrible trial, Therese supposed that it was given to her so that she might know the state of those men and women living in the world who cannot believe in God, who have no knowledge of Him, and who live in darkness as a result.

Such suffering is perhaps the very hardest to endure. Therese certainly found it so. Yet she did not give in to despair, but carried on the same practices, the same sacrifices, the same offerings as before. Her prayer life continued as before, though without any feeling that God was actually there, listening to her.

In her extremity, we know that she was even tempted to thoughts of suicide, for in one part of her autobiography she warns against placing any poison within the reach of a sick, suffering person. Such a temptation might prove too great, she says, as though she too was attracted by the thought of death. Perhaps she was.

Her final days were filled with the worst possible pain, and although she seemed to endure it with equanimity, we know from others' descriptions that her illness extracted the last ounce of suffering from her exhausted frame.

At the very end, when she underwent the final approach of death, those around her noticed a great transformation.

Looking at her crucifix, she said, "Oh, I love Him! My God, I love You!"

At once Therese became peaceful and her face was filled with indescribable joy. Radiance and bliss spread across her features, erasing every sign of the long agony she had endured. Finally, she gave a little sigh, and died. She had entered heaven, and her great work was about to begin.

Her autobiography rapidly became a best-seller, and millions of people around the world began to pray to St Therese for healing miracles, which were prompt in being granted.

Today, St Therese is one of the most popular saints of all time, and countless people have followed her Little Way by allowing God to transform their everyday sufferings and trials into the priceless currency of Heaven.

I am one of those pilgrims, and it was St Therese who showed me the only way to turn apparently useless pain into treasure for God.

St Therese's relics regularly travel the world so that millions more may learn about her life and death, and be inspired to imitate her.

*

Reading the above short biography, you may wonder how on earth a young nun who lived more than a century ago in a very different society could have anything to teach the average man or woman today. Her life was so short, and her experiences so limited, that it may seem futile to study her teachings.

That may be the obvious reaction, but it would be a great mistake.

True, the environment in which Therese of Lisieux lived was highly rarefied. Today, most of us live in a much more complex world, and the Christian faith is followed by comparatively fewer people than in her day, especially in the West.

Yet this very special individual – this young woman who suffered from a terminal disease at a time when medicine was relatively primitive, and who chose to undergo a life of continual mortification – has a great deal to teach us

Some of her experiences, especially those of her final year in which she battled with the challenge of unbelief, are even more meaningful to us now than in her own day. We live in an age when so many have lost their Christian faith or have never been taught about it. Religion has been shoved to the back of the shelf to make way for the glittering, deceptive rewards of materialism.

Fifty years ago, daily life in the West was permeated with Christian teachings, even though they were often unspoken. Today, little of that underpinning remains. We are people who are deprived of meaning unless we deliberately search for it. In this search, this daily battle against entropy, Therese has much to teach us.

Therese's understanding of the value of willing sacrifice, of the way in which our own suffering can be transformed into acts of love that are supremely valued by God, grew in stages as she matured.

We see Therese learning, while still a very young child, that by making small sacrifices she will please Jesus. Because she loves Him and loves her family, who taught her this method, she is eager to offer up the little daily acts which are all she has to give Him.

To begin with, she has nothing to offer the Lord except the physical actions which her family constantly encourage her to carry out, just as they themselves do. Therese's parents and her sisters provide her with teachings and with examples, and the child happily copies them. Such seemingly insignificant acts are possible for everyone, no matter what their situation may be.

Then, later, comes the great revelation Therese receives on Christmas Eve, in 1886. With this, Therese begins the more difficult task of disciplining her emotions and behaviour. When she enters the convent, she will already be experienced in this form of offering, which – again – is open to all of us to imitate. Overcoming our unruly emotional life and forming the habit of self-denial is supremely necessary for each and every one of us, and Therese explains to us in her autobiography how she learned to do this.

Already trained in these disciplines, a third type of suffering is asked of Therese in the final year of her life: she is deprived of spiritual consolation whilst undergoing the trial of her horribly painful illness and decline. All mystics are put to this particular test, the Dark Night of the Soul, which St John of the Cross has described so well for us.

God does not ask everyone to experience this form of suffering, but sends it only to those who will benefit from it. The most modern description of this Dark Night is given to us by Mother Teresa of Calcutta, in her searingly honest diaries. Some of us will undergo it, some will be spared, but if it comes to us then we may be sure that it issues from the hand of God the Father, and that some definite good will be the result of our willing acceptance.

By looking at the ways in which Therese suffered, the physical, emotional and spiritual trials she endured and the means she used to transform that suffering, we too can begin to see how the patient and willing endurance of all the trials that the Lord sends – the daily carrying of our individual cross, in fact – transforms pain into treasure.

Chapter Three

Different types of suffering – and why some is unnecessary

When we read the lives of the saints, all too often we're presented with a seemingly impossible type of heroic virtue. Yes, we all see how terrible were the tortures endured by, for example, St. Lawrence – who was literally grilled to death above an open fire – and we realize that only the Holy Spirit could have given him the courage to endure it.

At the same time, however, most of us can't truly identify with such a brave saint. I know I would never have the courage to endure pain such as this. I suspect most people feel the same way, that such enormous courage is to be admired and marvelled at, but also that it would be quite impossible for us to imitate.

Thank God, we don't have to.

For He has, in His wisdom, given to each of us the cross which best fits us. He knows what we can do, and what would be quite beyond us. He understands that for each one of us, heroic endurance of suffering may take the form of quietly accepting and offering up all the great and small pains and problems that plague us every day.

You probably know the story of the man who complained to God that his cross was too big for him to carry.

"Very well," said God, "you may look at some other crosses and choose one for yourself."

Suddenly, a door appeared before the man. He opened it and found himself in a room full of crosses. Pleased that at last he could be rid of his own burden, he placed it on the floor and began to sort through the pile of crosses before him.

All were different. Some were light, some heavy; some had sharp points that irritated his skin, while others were smooth but very slippery, so that they could hardly be carried at all.

Eventually, the man realised that none of the alternative crosses would suit him. They were all uncomfortable, difficult and the made of the wrong material, or the wrong shape, or too awkward.

At last he turned to the cross on the floor. On picking it up and carrying it in his arms, he realized that in fact this was the cross that best suited him. God had known it all along!

And so it is for each one of us. We all have crosses, and they are all different shapes and sizes. What seems impossibly heavy to me might be rather light and easy for you to bear; your own cross, however, might be shaped in quite the wrong way for me to carry.

Our own individual burden of suffering is shaped to fit us. At times we may rebel and wish to cast it aside, but if we were able to choose our particular burden, we would find in the end that it is precisely that which we already have.

The key is acceptance.

When we accept our cross, our individual form of suffering that God has permitted us to bear, this is in fact a form of humility. We are saying, in effect, not my will, but Thy will, be done: and this humility allows us to obey freely whatever God will send us, knowing that it will ultimately be for our own benefit and for the benefit of others.

Once we have truly accepted that our suffering comes from God and is given to us for our own benefit – for we are sure to find our courage and determination increase the more we accept that cross as our own – we will indeed see that it is given so that our loving acceptance may benefit others.

How could this happen?

We know that bearing our trials with patience and good will sets an example that other people will see and notice. It may be that seeing us carrying our cross gives others the courage to bear their own burden with equanimity.

We Catholics know that there is another benefit, however. Humility, courage and fortitude are virtues, and when we are able to manifest them in our daily lives a very fine, spiritual energy is created by our willing endurance. The Church calls this endurance, this energy, by the name of "merit".

Of course, the person who most perfectly created this merit, and in the most abundant quantity, is Jesus Christ. By His sufferings on the cross, he brought into existence such an enormous treasury of merit that it is sufficient for each and every one of us to call upon in times of need.

Not only is that great, unquantifiable merit given freely to all who need it, Christ gave us the great gift of being able to contribute to that treasury. This gift is truly astonishing. However small our efforts may seem to us, however insignificant in the eyes of the world, Jesus Christ accepts our own offering just as He praised the widow who gave her only coin.

That is why, when we offer up our suffering each day, whether it be great or small, we can know that we are helping Christ in His great saving work. When we join our own sufferings to those He endured on the cross, the tiny part that we contribute is magnified and included with His, and becomes part of the great treasury that is used to save souls and lighten others' burdens.

The saving of a child's life, for example, may be due to the silent prayer of a contemplative nun on the other side of the world. The amount of merit that she creates from her constant endurance of convent life and the rigours of regular, lengthy prayer may tip the balance in favour of saving that unknown child's life.

In just the same way we, as we offer up our arthritis or our forbearance or our willing acceptance of some chore we would rather not undertake, are perhaps bringing a soul from a distant country a little closer to God. Possibly we, too, may be helping to heal a sick child or comfort a bereaved spouse. We don't know how our offering will be used.

If we wish, we may offer up our suffering, our obedience, for a cause we hold dear. If a family member is seriously ill, or there is a natural disaster somewhere in the world, or we are concerned about threats to world peace, for example, these causes can be held up to Christ along with our own cross. I have a friend who always pleads for the cause of animal welfare, in her case for a charity which looks after abused horses and donkeys. I am sure that Jesus, whose Word created the animals, accepts her plea with love.

We may be sure there are innumerable miracles, even as you read this, that are being enabled by the contribution of unknown men and women, people just like you and me, who patiently carry their cross and offer their sufferings to Jesus to use as He wishes.

Why this should be is a mystery. God could, of course, work miracles perfectly well without our help, but He has willed that our small efforts should count, should help Him in His own saving work.

As we become transformed by carrying our cross, so our own transformation helps others, helps God Himself.

What an enormous gift this is, and how seldom we think of it!

$$*\qquad*\qquad*$$

There are many types of suffering. For the purposes of this book, I'm going to group them into three main types so that we can look at their origin and see how best to deal with them.

Some sufferings are more physical, some more psychological. All will have elements of each, all have a place in our personal spiritual development, and all need to be understood and classified according to their nature.

In the rest of this book I am going to use the terms "necessary" and "unnecessary" suffering when considering the different forms we are all called upon to undergo in our personal pilgrimage towards God.

The unnecessary sufferings are those which - as the name tells us – we do not have to endure at all. They are not our own cross; they are not fruitful; they don't bring us closer to God. Our spiritual path begins by painstakingly becoming free of them, and it is only then that our "necessary" sufferings – our own personal cross – can be accepted and transformed.

The other crosses, those which are necessary for our development and which Jesus wishes us to offer to Him, consist, firstly, of the real suffering which comes to all of us because we live in a fallen creation; and, second, the pain and remorse we feel as we see ourselves as we really are, through the eyes of conscience.

A wise confessor will help us to forgive ourselves, and to know that we are forgiven by God. A discerning spiritual director will help us to distinguish the necessary from the unnecessary in our sufferings. She will lead us to see what we need to discard from our thinking and feeling, and what is real and vital for our spiritual development.

I believe that Dr Maurice Nicoll, the late Harley Street psychiatrist and writer on Christian spirituality, was the first to use the terms "necessary" and "unnecessary" suffering. Dr Nicoll synthesized the teachings of Christianity with the insights he gained from Jungian psychology and the system of psychological transformation he learned from George Gurdjieff and Pyotr Ouspensky known as "the Work".

The latter teachings are actually Christian in origin, although they have been adopted and often misapplied by various New Age writers. I have written more about the Work in an appendix to this book.

More recently Father Christopher Ngozi Onuoha, a priest who served in the Archdiocese of Omaha, and whose comprehensive teachings on suffering are contained in his book, "Healing You and Your Family Tree", also makes this distinction.

This insightful priest also discriminates between suffering that is necessary for our salvation, or for the salvation of others, and completely unnecessary suffering, which we impose on ourselves.

Fr. Onuoha writes, "Jesus did not suffer and die … so that we may undergo unnecessary suffering. His suffering and death were necessary so that we might be freed from unnecessary bondage".

On the other hand, he states that "Suffering that is necessary for salvation may not go away until the purpose for which it is allowed is accomplished."

As long as we remain mechanical in nature, reacting unthinkingly to all the big and small problems we face, we will suffer uselessly.

Father Onuoha and Dr Nicoll both provide a useful schema with which to look at the various categories of sufferings we all experience, and they explain the place and usefulness – or otherwise – of each. Father Onuoha writes from an explicitly

Catholic approach, while Dr Nicoll includes psychological insight he gained while studying with Jung. Both are useful in our quest to understand suffering.

The first type, our unnecessary suffering, is completely useless. Jesus does not wish us to suffer in this way, and if we ask Him, He gives us the power to be free of it. Such suffering is the type which we bring on ourselves by our negative attitudes, thoughts and feelings, and which bring no benefit at all to anyone.

We might also call this type of unnecessary suffering "neurotic". It springs from our deep-seated, largely unconscious, pathological reactions to people and events. Usually it has been created in us by events in childhood, and it is the cause of so much of our daily misery. It is a mechanical process that takes up our thoughts and feelings without any conscious input, and it is only when we see it for what it is that we can put a stop to it.

When we complain, when we feel sorry for ourselves, when we resent people or things around us – in short, when we rebel against our own particular cross, and try by various unhealthy means to be free of it – we are suffering unnecessarily.

It is this type of suffering which brings people to seek help from psychologists and counsellors, and the good news is that it can be reduced or eliminated altogether if we're prepared to put in the hard work of gaining insight and then changing our behaviour.

A good spiritual director can help us to see when counselling is needed, and will encourage us to find a sympathetic therapist, someone who will not belittle our spiritual endeavours but respect our faith as we try to deal with the various psychological obstacles which stand in the way of our practice.

I am not including in this category the type of mental illness which needs very specialized treatments, often including medication: various psychoses, free-floating anxiety, serious phobias such as agoraphobia, and obsessive compulsive behaviours which cause people severe stress.

Nor am I including addictions here, whether to alcohol, illegal drugs, sexual pathologies, eating disorders, and so on.

These are indeed unnecessary for our survival, so much so that they pose a threat to life. Every year many people all over the world die because of their addictions. Either their drug of choice, whether alcohol or other substances, directly kills them through an overdose, or they kill themselves deliberately because of the damage their drug has caused them. Some overdoses are accidental, and some are the result of a deliberate suicide.

We cannot change these sorts of illnesses by our own personal psychological work, but must seek help as soon as possible.

Addictions are very heavy crosses, both for addicts and for those who love them, and God does give the power to overcome them, if the addict is sincere in his or her wish to be free.

God does this through several means, the first of which is the Twelve Step programmes of Alcoholics Anonymous and Narcotics Anonymous, and now for several other types of addiction. In common with many others, I became healed of my own addiction to alcohol through attending AA, and practising the steps. Jesus used the power of the Steps to heal me. I wrote about this process in my previous book, "A Raging Thirst". I found that AA was all I needed to be completely healed, and its Christian spirituality helped me to find my way into the church.

For others, it may be necessary to undergo detox and to spend time in a rehabilitation centre. When they are ready to leave, they are strongly encouraged to attend Twelve Step meetings, and those who do so have the best chance of staying clean and sober. The addict or alcoholic who begins to live a spiritual life lays hold of God's healing power to remain free from addiction. Such miracles happen every day.

Most of us, fortunately, do not suffer from such severe mental problems.

Our own unnecessary suffering takes many forms, none of them fatal, but all inimical to personal happiness and our spiritual growth. They take us further away from God, and benefit no-one.

In this category we find such negative states as envy, or anger, or self-pity. Lust, too, comes under this heading, as does needless worry and anxiety. We may have faith in God, but somehow in our everyday lives this seems to recede into the background and the chattering monkey, the restless mind and heart, takes over and directs our thoughts.

Everyone has come across the sort of person who complains all the time about everything! They are never happy. They are the "glass half-empty" people, who know no peace because nothing is ever good enough.

Or we may consider the constantly angry person, the bullying boss, the resentful employee, the irritable spouse. To live with such anger is harmful both to the angry person and to those around them.

In our day, lust may take the form of internet pornography addiction, or compulsive sexual behaviours. Jesus Himself describes such a person when he warns that if you lust after someone in your heart, you are already committing adultery.

Fortunately, all these harmful feelings can be greatly helped by therapy if the sufferer really wishes to be free. We don't have to live with them, although the work needed to undo their grip can be very difficult. A Christian therapist who understands the different types of suffering, and the place of real suffering in our lives, will be invaluable here.

You may be fortunate to find such a person, but even without such help, a wise priest and confessor can do much to encourage you to battle with temptation. Reading the scriptures and the writings of saints who have undergone such trials is extremely helpful, and will reassure you that you are not alone in your trials.

Prayer, of course, is our number one weapon and resource to conquer unnecessary suffering. It should become a vital part of our life, and we shall look later in this book at ways to build prayer into our everyday routines.

Negative thoughts are just as dangerous for our well-being. We may be constantly suspicious, convinced that our loved one is unfaithful; or we may harbour thoughts of retribution against someone who has hurt us, and whom we refuse to forgive.

As counsellors say, we are not responsible for the first negative thought or feeling that we experience, but we are definitely responsible for the second! Once we become aware of our state of mind, we can choose what to focus on and what to let go. God helps us to do this, knowing that constant negativity cuts us off from Him. He will reach down and pull us out of any pit of negative thinking or feeling where we feel stuck.

Sometimes – perhaps only too often for some of us – a real, physical pain or illness can give rise to neurotic suffering. There is the unavoidable pain itself, which will be considered later in this book, but then there are the quite unnecessary but very painful mental states that can follow it.

Martin Laird, in his book "Into the Silent Land", notes that "Thoughts about pain are worse than pain by itself".

He tells the story of a devout Christian who suffered a sudden, painful disease that left her bedridden for much of the time. She learned the simple Jesus prayer described below, and found it a great consolation in taking her thoughts out of herself and her own suffering. She realized that she could distinguish the suffering of pain itself from the suffering caused by thoughts about the pain.

"Suffering is what your mind does with your pain," she told Laird. "A quiet mind knows no suffering."

What she meant was that physical pain can be borne if we simply allow it to happen. It is the mind's persistent rebellion and the dark moods into which it can lead us which make everything worse.

Returning to our own negative thoughts and feelings, I believe some may be demonic in origin. Self-pity, temptations towards harming oneself, and hatred or even simple mistrust of others are thoughts that may be floating around in our psychological atmosphere, placed there by Satan or one of his minions, waiting for someone to grab them and to act on them.

Again, a good spiritual director can help us to see what the origins of our personal sufferings may be. After we have observed our own mental habits for some time we can begin to understand the way they arise in us, and we may see for ourselves that some are so outside our normal way of thinking that a demonic source could well be responsible.

We don't need to be unduly alarmed if this is what we observe. The remedy is in our own hands, and includes regular prayer, especially during times of temptation. If we have already established a practice such as the Jesus Prayer, or praying the Rosary, we will find it a tremendous remedy for the heaviness or despair that can come upon any of us during times of difficulty. Keeping holy water to hand is also a wise habit, especially for people with chronic depression or physical illness who may be tempted to despair. St.Therese was herself tempted in this way.

If such feelings persist, it is important to ask the help of a priest who has experience in these matters.

Every Catholic diocese has access to a trained and accredited exorcist, whose skills include discernment, a careful consideration of possible supernatural involvement in suffering. Fortunately, this situation is extremely rare, despite the popularity of films about exorcists!

If it should prove there is a demonic element in your suffering, there is no need to be afraid. St Therese later said that she thought some of her temptations came from the devil, but prayer – especially to Jesus and to Our Lady – was most effective in conquering them.

When less deep-seated negative thoughts or feelings occur, it may be that all we need to do is to simply and quietly turn our thoughts to something else. More persistent and long-standing examples will need therapeutic help as well as prayer, as we noted earlier. There is no shame attached to needing help. Even Our Lord sought the comfort of His friends when in agony, in Gethsemane.

My own late spiritual director used to recommend the Jesus Prayer as a sovereign remedy for all negativity.

To practice this prayer, we mentally say "Lord Jesus Christ, Son of the Living God, have mercy on me, a sinner". As we pray the words, we observe our breath, and mentally pray the first half of the prayer as we breathe in; then in the same way we pray the second part as we breathe out.

Eventually, we find that we grow calmer and our breathing becomes perfectly synchronized with the words of the prayer.

Any Christian, of whatever denomination, can pray this ancient prayer with sincerity and assurance, and if we persist we will notice that we are growing calmer and that other thoughts have vanished.

Other forms of prayer may also be used, such as the short prayer "O Most Sacred Heart of Jesus, I place all my trust in

Thee"; or the opening sentence of the "Hail Mary" prayer.

All these have the benefit of raising our heart and mind towards heaven, and allow us to disengage our thoughts and feelings from the endless mind-chatter that brings such unhappiness and discontent.

All unnecessary suffering is covered by Dr Nicoll's assertion that *we have a right not to be negative.*

This statement is simple but profound.

Note that he does not say that we have no right to be negative. On the contrary, if we want to remain unhappy or unfulfilled, we have every right to do so! If we live constantly in a negative psychological state, however, it is impossible to make any spiritual progress.

There is, however, great merit in making efforts to be free from this form of suffering. If we honestly want to change, we will be prepared to put in the hard work it entails, and we will seek help from God to do so.

Writing from his perspective as a psychiatrist, Dr Nicoll emphasized that we need to know ourselves through and through before we can begin to change. Only in this way can mechanical reactions become conscious.

That knowledge, painful though it may be, is the only way we can see who we are and what we need to change in our thinking. And if we do not know our faults and our neuroses, we cannot ask God's help to change us.

Many saints and writers on Christian spirituality suggest we start each day with a period of contemplation. Regular meditation, or contemplation, will help us to collect our scattered thoughts and centre ourselves in God.

There are many methods of Christian meditation, my

favourite being the Centering Prayer described by Father Basil Pennington.

To practise it, we choose a word which helps us centre our thoughts on God. It could be the name of Jesus, or a simple word which we associate with peace. Some of the choices made by meditators have been "Father", "Ave Maria", "Peace" and "Love". It may be any word, however, as long as it helps you to calm your thoughts and centre them on the Lord.

We simply sit, with closed eyes, in a comfortable position and in a quite place, and mentally repeat our chosen word. Whenever we find that we have ceased to repeat it, we centre our thoughts upon it again and begin afresh.

How long we spend in meditation is up to each individual. Most experienced meditators find that 20 minutes is a suitable period, and it's useful to keep a clock or watch close by so that you may easily check the time. It will not harm your meditation if you simply open your eyes and look at the clock face.

At the end of our meditation it is helpful to pray the Lord's Prayer, either silently or aloud. Then we open our eyes and calmly go about our business.

We will find that as our thoughts grow calmer and our emotions become peaceful, we are given the energy to face the day with all its challenges, knowing that we can return – if just for a minute or two – to the quiet, calm centre where we meet with Christ.

During the day, such "returns" are reference points for us. We take a minute to observe ourselves and the thoughts and feelings which are occupying our mind at that moment; then, placing them to one side, we allow the deep peace we felt in the morning meditation to flood our consciousness for a short time.

Often we will find we complicate our own lives with unnecessary suffering. We are always going to experience problems in our daily lives, but as long as we protest – even if just to ourselves – we are adding to our own difficulties.

With observation, we may find we harbour negative thoughts which haunt us and spoil our efforts to accept our circumstances, including not only any pain or physical problems but the psychological effects on us of the people around us.

Why, we wonder, has God sent us this or that difficult neighbour – the crosspatch, the grumbler, the noisy teenager next door? Or our perfectionist boss, who is never satisfied with our work? Even those we love most of all can be hard to live with. Sometimes they may be the hardest of all to accept, because they are so often present, along with their particular irritations.

St Therese describes a particular nun who used to spoil silent prayer times by clicking on her rosary. Another sister would always manage to splash Therese's face with filthy water from washing handkerchiefs whenever they shared laundry duty.

It is not the act itself, or the experience of a problem, which is so difficult to bear, but the way our minds object to having it. When we stop objecting and decide to accept whatever God has given us in that particular moment, we find our problems suddenly lighten, until they become just another experience in our everyday lives – neither good nor bad, just present, to be patiently accepted or acted upon, as the situation demands.

Acceptance is the acknowledgement that we cannot change everything to our liking. It is the attitude we need to have if we are to acquire serenity, as the famous prayer puts it.

The "Serenity Prayer" has become well known all over the world through its use by Alcoholics Anonymous and other 12-Step programmes. Its usefulness is not restricted to those struggling with addiction, however. Its simple but profound words show us the key to becoming serene, accepting our lives and the people in them as they are, and making peace with them.

In it, we ask God for the right attitude to whatever is troubling us, and for help to accept what is going on in our lives, however hard it may be.

It says:

"God,
Grant me the serenity to accept the things I cannot change,
The courage to change the things I can,
And the wisdom to know the difference."

This is the prayer that has become so popular you can even find it on tea towels! Yet, easy as it is to read, it is often very difficult to practise. The more we make the effort to acquire the qualities it asks God to give us, the more tranquil our lives will become, as unnecessary suffering fades into the background and no longer dictates our thoughts and feelings.

All our sincere endeavours to know ourselves and to change our habitual negativity may be offered to God in this prayer, and we can be sure that He will bless them and enable us to succeed.

The type of suffering I have described as "unnecessary" may be called our "false cross". It is false because it is not given to us by God, and we do not need to carry it. There is no merit in complaining, rebelling, growing resentful or filling ourselves with self-pity, as our negativity can lead us to do.

The Serenity Prayer calls on us to change the things that we can, and that includes, of course, the "false cross" we carry, composed of our habitual negativity. We can change that very simply, by acknowledging these thoughts and feelings and separating ourselves from them. It is a vital work, but impossible without God's help.

When we take this step, we begin to understand that our negativity makes us a burden to ourselves when we think and behave in this way, and that we also become a burden to others.

No doubt you will be able to think of many examples of false crosses, both your own and those of other people.

A prime example for me was someone I knew well, an often very sweet and kind-hearted older lady who was unfortunately given to self-pity. No matter how a conversation might start, it all too frequently ended with her lament that, "I should never have left my home town."

All her troubles, she declared, could be traced back to the "mistake" she had made forty years earlier when she moved away from the small town where she had grown up. That she had done so willingly, in order to marry the man she loved, was forgotten in the complaint she so often made.

Of course, this attitude, this objection, was quite useless as well as wrong. Her problems came from her mechanical habit of feeling sorry for herself, but when she stopped focusing on her own negative feelings she became the kind and helpful person she too seldom was.

Self-pity, aided and abetted by nostalgia, was her false cross, and it became a real cross for those around her who loved her, yet were forced to listen to this oft-repeated lament.

She refused to consider therapy or medical help, and by shutting herself off from this, she remained unhappy and resentful all her life. Her true character, that of a thoughtful and sympathetic friend, shone out all too rarely.

We have all felt self-pity and resentment towards people and things which we find annoying. Through paying close attention to the sequence of thoughts and feelings that accompany us throughout the day, we may discover that so many problems stem from an underlying attitude that Dr. Nicoll calls "making requirements".

Requirements are the unconscious demands we place upon other people and the world in general. We *require* that everyone should treat us with respect. We *require* that buses and trains run on time. We *require* that our work should go well, and that our family should be loving and considerate at all times. We *require* so many things, in fact, that we can never be satisfied, because those requirements will never be met!

Dr Nicoll doesn't say we should always put up with harsh words or ill treatment – definitely not. At times we will have to take action to protect ourselves from the ill-will of others. But having requirements means that we expect that all our wants will be met, and that people should always and in all conditions show us the politeness and respect that we would prefer and that we secretly think is our due.

Again, this particular approach to life shows a lack of humility. Why should everything be done to please us? Are we more important than other people? Of course not!

The problem of requirements also explains why so many people, when facing sudden setbacks or unexpected suffering, ask "Why should this happen to me?"

The only possible answer is another question – why not? Why shouldn't we all have our share in suffering, since this is the condition of living in a fallen world? And especially when we, as Christians, are given suffering as a means of transformation and purification.

Suffering is not something to be shunned or feared, although most of us do react in this way when it appears in our lives. It offers us the road to draw closer to God and to take a small part in the saving work of Jesus; what is more, we never have to face it alone.

If we look deeper into our Christian faith and read the Gospels more often, we will be reminded that Jesus desires to bear all our burdens for us.

"Come unto me, ye who are weary and heavy laden, and I will give you peace," He tells us. "My yoke is easy, and my burden is light."

Indeed this is true. When we find ourselves in a state of self-pity, resentment, anger or whatever our own habitual negative thoughts and feelings may be, all we need do is turn to Jesus. We can visualize our unnecessary suffering as a bundle of old sticks, and then see ourselves placing this untidy, uncomfortable and useless package at His feet.

He will take it from us, and stretch out His loving arms to draw us closer to his breast. And we will see our old, outgrown bundle of care roll away, down the hill, away from us – gone at last; or at least, until the next time we find ourselves picking it up again.

Through observing ourselves and getting to know our habits of feeling and thinking, we learn to sense earlier and earlier when we are in danger of accumulating such a bundle. Eventually, we grow so tired of carrying it that we are able to let it go before it becomes a problem. We see and feel these harmful thoughts long before they actually start to drag us down, and as soon as we do, we turn to Jesus and away from ourselves.

As evangelist Joyce Meyer says, we can all learn to "cast our care" upon the Lord, instead of carrying it all by ourselves.

In time, we find our false cross ceases to burden us, and we in turn are no longer a burden to others.

We recall that Jesus said to Martha, when that hard-working friend complained about being left to do all the work while her sister, Mary, sat at His feet, that it was Mary who had chosen the better part.

I have always felt sorry for Martha, who was, as some translations say, "much cumbered about" with serving. We are all, at times, much cumbered about – mentally and physically –

and yet, if we only take a moment to stop our burdensome attempts to serve, and instead turn our attention to listen to the Lord as He speaks to us, we will find ourselves miraculously refreshed and freed to do the real work that Christ wants us to do.

Martha's error was not that she carried out the practical tasks needed to entertain their guest, but that she did so at the wrong time – when she could have listened to the Lord instead of working.

What was even worse, she was carrying a false cross, that of resentment. She was angry that her sister was not helping her, and her anger stood in the way of seeing that she herself needed to sit at the feet of Jesus, just as Mary was doing, and learn from the Lord.

Father Onuoha calls this attitude "victim mentality syndrome".

This particular false cross causes pain and suffering because we wrongly think we are being unfairly treated. At times this may be true, but it is a good practice, should these resentful thoughts arise, to ignore them and turn to Jesus to see what He is saying about our situation. We may find that, far from being victims, we are beneficiaries of a golden opportunity to learn something about ourselves and about God.

We might think that great saints, the type who underwent tremendous real suffering, were never troubled by these false crosses, these unreal burdens, the unnecessary suffering I have been describing.

Yet, looking again at the life of St Therese, we see that during her childhood and early adolescence she too experienced this type of suffering.

We're unaccustomed to thinking of great saints in terms of everyday, neurotic, unnecessary suffering. By the time they have reached sainthood, only their real, heroic sufferings are part of their story. Most of them have left little record of their earliest years, but they too are human, and surely went through all that we ourselves undergo.

Because St Therese is so close to us in time and her autobiography so honest, however, we can see how the young saint exhibited psychological problems that we would call neurotic, the product of her early deprivations and fractured family life. She knew she was unhappy, both at home, after the death of her mother, and at school, where she could not make herself fit in with the average pupil and felt lonely and miserable.

During her childhood illness, which was probably at least partly demonic in origin, she experienced much unhappiness and was consoled only by the Virgin's loving smile as she lay in bed. Eventually, the nervous attacks and nightmares ceased, and she returned to normal life, but she was still immature and was troubled by anxiety and even depression.

Only on the fateful Christmas Eve when Therese heard her father complain about her childishness did this miasma of neuroticism and sheer unhappiness lift from her.

Among French families at this time it was customary for children to leave their shoes out so that Baby Jesus would fill them with sweets and little gifts.

Therese was really past the age for this, but – perhaps in order to please her father, who liked to treat her as even younger than she was – the family continued with the ritual each year.

That particular Christmas Eve, M. Martin was tired and out of temper, and Therese heard him to say to her sister Celine, "Therese ought to have outgrown this sort of thing, and I hope this will be the last time."

What a shock it must have been to Therese, who loved her

father with all her heart, and who thought he enjoyed babying her, to hear these harsh words!

Yet, here the miracle took place – for, contrary to Celine's expectation, and in complete contrast to her previous childishness – Therese put on a brave face, and played the part of a delighted little girl, just as if she had not heard her father's complaint.

Running downstairs, she knelt by the fire and unwrapped her little presents as if nothing had happened.

Celine was amazed, but Therese knew that she had just experienced the great grace of an everyday miracle. For years she had struggled with her feelings, her need to be constantly affirmed and assured of her father's love, yet she had not been able to break free from this bondage.

All at once, God had reached down from Heaven and, Therese said, "The Divine Child, scarcely an hour old, flooded the darkness of my soul with radiant light".

Jesus Himself, she later said, had done for her what years of trying had failed to achieve. In one instant, her neuroses were healed. She had given her burden to the Lord, and He had exchanged it for an experience of great bliss.

All her efforts had seemed to get nowhere, but secretly, in the depths of Therese's soul, her formation had been taking place in silence, and unknown to her.

This is often the way of spiritual progress. It can seem for long periods that we are making no headway at all and are just as selfish, just as much a burden to ourselves and others, as we were at the outset.

The young Therese shows us that, if we are ready to relinquish our unnecessary suffering, our neurotic and unhealthy thoughts and feelings, and if we make what efforts we can, God can step in and in the space of a moment fill us with the grace we need to break free of such heavy bondage.

Sometimes this happens all at once, as with St. Therese; sometimes it is given to us in small enlightenments and understandings, perhaps with the help of a spiritual director or counsellor, when we suddenly experience an "Aha" moment. We see in a flash that it was we ourselves to whom we were enslaved, our own sinful nature, our own addictions. And with that insight comes freedom.

For most of us, the insight will need to be built upon daily and recalled often in times of temptation. Only rarely does the change prove so cataclysmic that it is not necessary to revisit the old attitudes. But whether it happens swiftly or slowly, we will find that with prayer our freedom grows, and grace continues to work in us, and miracles occur.

When you give up your unhealthy, unnecessary suffering, you enable God to work those miracles deep within your soul. You allow Him to shape you into the person He always knew you to be, the loving soul who follows Him faithfully and carries her cross, the cross which will be transformed by Him into a gift of tremendous value.

When you give up your false cross, your false currency, you will be free to bear your real cross. Yes, it will bring suffering, but your true cross, when accepted and borne with courage, will bring tremendous joy and life-saving power to you and to others.

As you accept your cross, you will necessarily become purified in the cleansing fire that suffering brings. This is exactly the same process that we shall all undergo in Purgatory if we die with negative thoughts, selfish tendencies and attitudes. After all, we can't hope to enter Heaven with a mind full of requirements, resentments and objections! A place where such difficulties exist would not be Heaven at all.

We must change, or rather, allow ourselves to be changed, so that in releasing our false crosses we grow strong enough to carry our real cross, whatever that may turn out to be.

Without God, real change is not possible.

With Him, everything is possible.

Chapter Four

Unavoidable suffering – physical, emotional and spiritual

Previously, we looked at the role of unnecessary suffering in our life, and we saw that we may be free of it if we remember to turn to Jesus. He has promised to bear our burdens, and He is faithful to keep His promises. There is no merit in the suffering we endure because of our own psychological attitudes. On the contrary, we please the Lord when we make efforts to be free of it.

Once we give up our false cross, we are much better able to carry our real cross, the suffering which comes to us unbidden and through which we may share in God's redemptive work on Earth.

This is a great privilege. God has willed that when we bear our own cross, we not only allow Him to transform us through suffering, we are also given the opportunity to help Him. No other creature shares this privilege; it is unique to human beings.

The cross we ourselves are given is ours alone. Nobody else has one quite like it. It suits us perfectly, and God will always give us the grace to bear it as long as we turn to Him and ask for that grace.

It will not be easy. We are fallen beings, liven in a fallen world, and we are inevitably going to experience suffering, whether physical, mental or spiritual. Sometimes we will find our suffering contains two or even all three of these elements. In times of darkness we may fear we are too weak to carry it, and may pray – as Jesus did in Gethsemane – that our suffering may be taken away.

Our Lord took upon Himself the heaviest cross the world has

ever known, and He suffered much more than anyone else has been, or ever will be, asked to endure.

Because He was fully human as well as fully divine, He knew very well that He was going to undergo a terrible ordeal. Perhaps he was literally terrified. We are told that He "sweated blood" as he prayed in that garden, and yet, ultimately, He found the courage and grace from His Father that enabled Him to endure to the end.

We must thank God that we will never have to face anything like the Cross of Jesus.

In the following three chapters I want to look more closely at exactly what Christ went through; to put our own sufferings into some perspective, I will ,look at the actual events of the crucifixion and how they affected Our Lord. He suffered in every possible way, and because He did so, we may be sure that there is nothing in our lives too painful, too difficult, for Him to help us to bear it. He knows exactly what we are going through, because He did so Himself.

After understanding what Jesus suffered on the cross – physically, emotionally and spiritually – we will look at what sort of cross we ourselves are asked to carry.

Then we will see what St Therese suffered, and how she used her own pain to unite her sufferings with those of Christ; when she did so, she found a way to work with Jesus in bringing souls to salvation, and at the same time to become ever more closely united with Him in her heart.

These sufferings are part of what the Serenity Prayer calls "the things I cannot change". By practising prayer and acceptance as part of our daily spiritual discipline, we become more aware of the need to change what we can; with this as our background, we are able to look more closely at the things we cannot change.

We need to bear in mind that when we are firmly rooted in our love for God, and trying to become the person He intends us to be, everything that happens to us is part of His will for us. No matter how painful or difficult it may be, each situation, each event, is part of our pilgrimage towards Heaven.

And each pain, each burden, willingly borne by us becomes a precious treasure that we may offer Him each day.

*   *   *

First, let us consider the physical suffering that Jesus endured for us.

After Jesus was arrested He was taken to the Sanhedrin, the official court of the corrupt Jewish priesthood. The ordinary Jews, the crowds who followed Him every day to listen to His teachings, loved Jesus. They saw in Him a great Rabbi, possibly the very person who would liberate them from the Roman occupation. Some were beginning to assert that Jesus was the Messiah, and the Jewish priests – led by the Chief Priest, Caiaphas – were afraid it might be true.

Many of the so-called temple priests were not even fully Jewish, but came from families who had intermarried over many years with non-Jewish, powerful families. It is important for us to know this, because many anti-Semites have used the Biblical account of the trial of Jesus to call Jews deicides, killers of God, and this is far from the truth.

As Saint John Paul II pointed out, the crowds who later called for Jesus to be killed were stirred up by the Chief Priest's minions. They may well have been drunk; they were certainly ill-informed and fearful of punishment from the priests, who had power to excommunicate them, and from the Romans, who could kill them if they disobeyed Roman law.

To lead a crowd against Roman rule was the worst form of

disobedience, and these crowds, in fear of their lives, disavowed any association with Jesus.

And, as Saint John Paul II also rightly said, the Jews who actually did call for Jesus to be killed were not only ignorant – as the Lord Himself said from the cross - they were relatively few in number, and the charge of murder could not be laid at their descendants, much less ascribed to all Jews, as countless anti-Semites have claimed over the millennia.

To picture the scene, then, let us imagine Jesus as He stood before Caiaphas. He refused to answer Caiaphas, and was struck across the face for doing so. The palace guards then bound Him to a pillar, spat in His face, and pulled on His beard. Spitting was among the most insulting acts possible, and pulling the beard of a rabbi not far behind.

Disgraced and shamed, Jesus was taken first to Pilate, the Roman procurator, and then – when Pilate found no fault in Him – to Herod, the evil king, who came from a non-Jewish family but who ruled over the Jews under Pilate.

Herod could apparently find no fault in Him, and returned him to Pilate. It is then that the procurator offered to release Jesus, as it was the custom to release one prisoner to the Jews at the time of Passover. The crowds – stirred up, as we have seen, by the guards of the Chief Priest and the Roman soldiers – and frightened for their own lives, demanded that Jesus be crucified. Pilate released Barabbas, the other prisoner at that time, and the torture and crucifixion of Jesus began in earnest.

Jesus was stripped of his clothes and tied to a pillar. As the soldiers gambled for possession of His garment, He was struck again and again with a heavy leather thong, until His skin was cut and bleeding. Such flagellation is truly torture, for it results in long strips of skin being pulled off, and the flesh beneath exposed to more pain.

Eventually, when the soldiers saw that Jesus was truly

exhausted and half-dead, they placed a crown of thorns upon His head.

If you have ever seen the thorn bushes that grow in the Middle East, you will know that they are not the relatively tame thorns that we know here in the West.

The thorns that comprised the crown of Jesus were over an inch long and as sharp as needles; as the crown was pressed down upon His head, deep furrows were scraped in His skin and blood poured down upon His face.

At last it was time for the crucifixion.

We know that Jesus was too weak to carry His own cross for long, and that a passer-by, probably from among the crowds that loved Him and were horrified at what was happening, reached out and shouldered the cross himself.

Tradition has it that this stranger, Simon of Cyrene, was a black man, and that is how he is always depicted. The Jews were not a completely homogeneous crowd, as although they were mostly related to one another they also accepted converts from other nations. St Simon, as he is now known, may well have come from North Africa in order to be in Jerusalem for the Passover; whilst there, he could have been among the devoted crowds who listened every day to Jesus in the temple.

When the actual crucifixion began, Jesus was nailed to the cross by the skin and bones just above His hands and by His feet. This posture would have caused dreadful, fiery pains to shoot along His chief nerves and into His brain, adding to the unimaginable torture that He already suffered.

As the crucifixion continued, great cramps would have clenched His muscles, making Him unable to push Himself higher. From time to time He would have been able to raise Himself slightly in order to breathe, but this relief would have been short-lived.

Between the waves of agony convulsing the Lord's body, He uttered the seven last words from the cross. Finally, the death throes began, and Jesus cried out, "It is finished."

The Lord gave up His life, in the most appalling pain possible, and His mission on Earth was complete.

Normally a death by crucifixion would have taken two or three days to complete, but in the case of Jesus, because He was already so weakened by the loss of blood, and so dehydrated, His body gave up His life much sooner. We are told it took about six hours for Him to die, and when the Roman soldiers came to check on the progress of their victims, they found Jesus was already dead.

In all this terrible process, there would not have been any part of the Lord's body which was not drenched in agony. Not a muscle, not a nerve but would have been flooded with unimaginable suffering. Truly, there is no pain we can feel in our own bodies that Jesus Himself did not suffer in His torture and death.

*　　*　　*

Physical pain is the most urgent of all sufferings. We can do nothing when we are in great physical pain, except – if we can remember – to offer our suffering to God.

I am not minimising the seriousness of other types of pain. We will look at emotional and spiritual pain in subsequent chapters. Once our physical pain is alleviated, at least to the point where we can think and feel again, we will be able to confront those other forms of suffering. But first, we must find ways to handle the pain of our body.

On the cross, pain penetrated every cell of Christ's own body,

55

the Precious Body that is offered once again to the Father, every time that Mass is said. Very seldom will such sufferings be repeated in our own lives; great saints and martyrs may indeed have lived through a similar agony, but we may thank God that we are not called to experience the same.

And yet, whatever our physical pain may be, whether it is as slight as a splinter in the hand or as agonising as a full-blown migraine or a broken limb, we too may offer it to the Father even as we seek ways to alleviate it.

I have experienced great pain at a certain time in my life, as I have described in my memoir "A Raging Thirst", and touched on in the preface to the present book.

My nerves were literally torn and my bones, from pelvis to ankles, were shattered. In addition a punctured lung, ruptured bladder, and numerous deep cuts and bruises added to the agony I felt.

When I had to be transferred from a stretcher to a hard surface so that X-Rays could be taken, my flesh felt literally as though it was on fire. I would never have believed that the human body could feel such pain and survive.

St. Therese made a similar observation in the last months of her life, and for her, the sufferings she felt were compounded by the fact that her Mother Superior refused to let her take pain-killers.

Today, we regard such withholding as barbaric. As a Benedictine priest once remarked to me, Christ has given scientists the ability to create pain-killers, and we need never forego them in the name of some abstract and wrong notion of suffering.

In any case, however, pain-killers have their limitations. While they do take away our physical pain they may also cloud our judgement and limit our ability to think and feel.

Yet, so does pain itself, and as I found, it does so in much greater degree. I use pain-killers daily, to remedy my physical suffering, and I give thanks to God for the genius of the doctors and researchers for making this possible.

Jesus Himself lived in an age when pain-killers were very weak, if they helped at all. The "sop" He was offered on the cross was probably some sort of diluted vinegar solution aimed at helping His thirst, but it may also have contained a primitive form of pain-killer such as willow bark or alcohol. He refused it, because He knew He had to go through this extreme agony so that He could achieve His extraordinary task – the redemption of mankind.

By suffering in this way, Jesus demonstrated the extent of His love for us. He consented to endure such agony because it was necessary so that He could complete the Divine Plan.

The physical agony shows us in a very concrete way just how much the Lord suffered on the cross. Yes, the emotional and spiritual sufferings were tremendous, but they are harder to understand unless we also have some prior concept of God, sacrifice and redemption. The pains the Lord felt in His body, however, can be understood by anyone who has ever suffered even the slightest physical pain.

The cross and the suffering that Jesus endured show us in immediately comprehensible terms just how far the love of God is prepared to go to redeem us. We may guess at another person's emotional suffering, and even empathise to some extent with spiritual pain. But physical suffering requires no guesswork. We see it take place and we know within our own body what that suffering entails, because we too have suffered physical pain.

Jesus chose to suffer so that we might be redeemed, and His sufferings were foreshadowed in the Old Testament. If there had been another way to bring about our redemption, God could have chosen to protect His Son from the agony of the cross, but there was none. This was the plan of salvation, the only path that would lead to redemption, since Adam and Eve first disobeyed in the Garden of Eden. Nothing less would accomplish it.

Mystically, the sufferings of Christ created tremendous spiritual power. His merit is limitless. It is that store, that treasury, of merit which is the priceless currency of Heaven.

The miracle is that, when we offer our own physical sufferings to God in prayer, we too are taking part in that mystical plan. Our willingness to offer up our pain is added to the spiritual treasury which Christ created for us. It is a tiny contribution to the work of redemption, in which Christ graciously allows us to take part.

Admittedly, as human beings our first reaction to physical pain may not be to turn to God. Whenever there is a physical pain, especially if it is severe, we first wish to be rid of it. Far from being grateful to the Lord for allowing us to participate in His suffering, we probably feel angry and emotionally hurt that He has burdened us with this cross.

It may take many days, months or even years before we are able to resign ourselves to pain, let alone to reach a state of equanimity and eventual gratitude.

I spent several months in hospital, during which my pain was often acute, and the most effort I could make was simply to keep breathing and praying for relief. It was only towards the end of that stay that I discovered St Therese and her profound teaching on suffering, and then I came to see how my pain could actually help me draw closer to God.

Even today, I may react with anger and disappointment when a new pain arises. Recently, on top of my neuropathy and chronic arthritis, I began to feel pain in my muscles, as well as in my bones and certain nerve endings. By now I have been practising the morning offering for many years, but still my physical body rebels at each new, unexpected setback.

Those years of practice help me tremendously, but I can't perform a "spiritual bypass" and simply accept everything that hurts, without a moment of anger – I must patiently work through the complex emotions that physical pain often brings. Only when I have done so can I reach acceptance. And acceptance is the necessary first stage to making pain an offering.

One of the problems with human suffering is that we project our pain into the future, and imagine what our lives will be like if there is no end to it. This is the wrong approach, however. We can live only one day at a time, and are given grace to endure for that period alone. We cannot have tomorrow's bread today. Jesus has told us not to indulge in this type of projection when he says that tomorrow will take of itself, and yet we so often forget this.

In Twelve Step programmes there are constant reminders that we must "keep it in the day". "One day at a time" is a commonly heard saying in AA and similar groups, because as human beings capable of imagining the future we are all too prone to worry about the future.

The Israelites were given only enough manna for each day when they wandered in the desert; if they tried to keep it overnight it went putrid and had to be thrown away. In the same way, we are to live fully today with all the resources that God gives us, and to trust that His grace will sustain us in the future just as it is doing today.

Keeping this in mind spares us many of the gloomy forebodings that can afflict us in times of illness.

"What if this goes on forever?"

"How can I possibly endure this another day?"

And, with great poignancy, when pain afflicts someone we love, "Suppose she has to live with this pain for years?"

These and other fears, though perfectly real, truly have no place in the Christian attitude to suffering. If we, or someone we love, is to suffer in the future, then we may expect that God will give us, or the other person, the grace and strength that would be needed in order to endure the trial. But we cannot foretell the future.

None of us knows what tomorrow holds. Perhaps there will be a miraculous cure, perhaps not. We, or our loved one, may die in our sleep. Or Jesus may return tomorrow morning! We literally do not and cannot know the future, and worry, while understandable, is quite useless.

Looking back to the previous chapter, in which we examined unnecessary suffering, we can see that anxiety, worrying about the future and about our ability to endure difficult circumstances of any sort, is a good example of suffering that brings no reward.

I know from my own experience that when we experience pain, we need only to endure it for that particular moment, that particular day. We can't suffer yesterday or tomorrow. We can only suffer today.

Most importantly, it is only in the day itself that we may offer our suffering to God.

I cannot offer Him tomorrow's pain, for it is unreal; I can offer only that which I am undergoing now, in this exact moment. That pain is real, and that is what we may offer, uniting it to the suffering of Jesus at Calvary, from love of Him and because we know that doing so is pleasing to Him; it allows us to work with Him in the salvation of souls and the comforting of others who suffer.

In his book "Into the Silent Land", Martin Laird quotes from someone suffering great pain and disability every day.

She had previously learned Christian contemplation, and found that when she was in pain she found relief in watching her breath and mentally reciting a simple prayer word.

Such a word or short phrase, which meditators repeat silently during their contemplation, may be used by anyone as an "arrow prayer". We should choose a word with spiritual meaning, such as "Jesus, Mercy" or "Ave Maria". There are many possibilities, as long as it is something that will remind you of the love and care of God.

Contemplation is a simple practice, and to have a background of regular contemplative prayer is a great help to anyone suffering from pain. You will find at the end of this book an appendix giving easily followed instructions in case you wish to practise this type of prayer, but it is not necessary to have such a background in order to choose a simple prayer word or phrase.

The practice of attention in pain consists of allowing one's breathing to occur naturally without any forcing, and paying attention to the breath as it happens. Then the prayer word can be said in silence, if possible following the rhythm of the breath.

That sounds much harder than it actually is.

I found this practice tremendously helpful when my pain was so intense that I could barely think at all. I placed my attention on my breathing, and mentally uttered the short Jesus Prayer, which is known all over the Christian world as a very effective meditation prayer.

The words are "Jesus, Son of the Living God, have mercy on me, a sinner".

In the traditional practice, the meditator recites the first part on the prayer whilst breathing in, and the second on the out breath.

Such a practice, which I learned from my spiritual director, comes from the Orthodox Tradition, but is entirely appropriate for any Christian to pray, at any time.

In times of intense physical suffering, we may shorten it to the simple words mentioned earlier, saying "Jesus, Mercy", if possible in synchrony with the breath.

If we prefer, we might pray the opening salutation of the Hail Mary prayer: "Hail Mary, full of grace, the Lord is with thee".

The patient mentioned by Martin Laird observed that, in her experience, "A silent mind knows no suffering."

What she meant was that the physical pain was still present, but the mind was not complicating it with anxiety, anger, fear or any other negative thoughts or emotions.

Pure suffering, then, is far easier to bear when we keep it entirely in the moment, and mental prayer together with attention to the breath is the best method I know for quieting the chattering mind.

When we allow the mind to stay silent before our pain, we discover that we are no longer a victim of the pain, but a witness to it.

We may come to realize that in this silence we become one with all who are suffering, wherever they may be, and simultaneously experience the Presence of God.

Such a great blessing is possible when we allow the pain to take place while we focus our attention on God.

Laird comments, "If (the patient) could be silent within

herself, in the midst of her pain, and not get caught up in commenting on the pain . . . what she found, even in the midst of this pain, was communion with all people in the silence of God."

What a tremendous gift this is for anyone who is suffering! God brings the greatest good out of what would otherwise be evil. He grants us the privilege of communion with Himself and with all who suffer, together with the knowledge that our own offering is infinitely precious to Him, little though it may seem to us.

Anyone who suffers in any way from physical pain may test this method for themselves.

The next time you experience pain of any sort, no matter how great or small, offer it up to God. Tell Him that you make this offering to Jesus so that He may unite it with His own suffering on the cross.

And then leave the burden with Him.

Practise the breathing exercise I have described, along with a sacred word of your own choosing.

Then, allow your mind to become still and to know God.

*   *   *

We saw in Chapter 2 that St Therese experienced every form of suffering possible. She entered Carmel knowing that physical suffering would be her lot, and that she would please Jesus by accepting whatever type of mortification He would choose to send her.

The nuns were always cold in winter. Nuns went without socks, in the same type of sandals that St Teresa of Avila and her own nuns had worn in the far warmer climate of Spain. The cold was a real trial to the young Therese, yet she never once complained or asked for a mitigation to the rule.

Thinking that Therese was in good health and would be happy to eat leftover food which none of the other nuns wanted, this was what they gave her at many mealtimes. Fish heads, cold vegetables, all sorts of unwanted and really unappetising morsels filled her plate, and they caused her much suffering.

From reading a list of her symptoms, it seems possible that Therese suffered from Irritable Bowel Syndrome. This condition would have caused her to suffer stomach cramps, wind and indigestion when eating these wholly unsuitable foods, but she never once protested or asked for anything different. To follow the Rule of the convent was her only aim, because she believed that any suffering that resulted from her obedience must have been willed by God, and so would be pleasing to Him.

Her stomach pains and cramps were only the beginning of Therese's physical sufferings, however.

As her tuberculosis progressed, she grew weaker and her lungs occasionally bled profusely. This, she thought, was a positive sign, because it meant she was on her way towards Heaven, towards Jesus, and that her time on earth would be short.

During her final year, Therese's sufferings were at their very worst. Other parts of her body were affected, and her bowel began to decay, even to the extent of an agonising gangrene setting in. She could keep little food down, and was unable to receive the Eucharist because her stomach would not allow her to retain even this heavenly food.

Her whole body was racked with pain.

In the final months of her life, Therese began to tell her fellow nuns about the extreme pains she was experiencing.
After one particularly harsh night, she confided, "Never did I

think I could suffer so much! But He will not abandon me."

Once, she asked a fellow nun to remind her of the benefits of suffering.

"When I say I am suffering," she requested the sister, "just respond by saying 'so much the better.'"

They practised this response for some time, as St Therese pushed her deteriorating body to take a few steps in the sick-room. At last she could manage no more, and knew she had reached the ultimate stage of suffering for that day.

Again, she told a group of nuns, "Oh, if you knew what I am going through. Tonight, when I could endure it no longer, I asked the Blessed Virgin to take my head in her hands, so that I could endure this pain. Oh, how I pity myself! Nevertheless, I would not suffer less."

If she had been given morphine, she would doubtless have taken it as long as it was in obedience to her Mother Superior. But the latter would not countenance it, and although the doctor had prescribed it, this relief was withheld from Therese.

Towards the very end, racked with pain in every part of her body, Therese confessed that the agonies had driven her to consider how welcome the idea of suicide might be to someone less focused on God.

"I assure you," she said, "that it takes only a moment to lose one's control when one has such pain."

She added that she would never have asked God to give her such suffering.

"I should never ask God for greater pain, for then it would be my own pain," she explained. "Then I would have to bear it alone, and I have never been able to do anything else."
Since – unlike many men and women in religious life, even

in our own day – Therese had eschewed such mortifications as wearing a hair shirt, or whipping herself, she knew that her sufferings had come from God alone. She also knew that if He sent her such agony, He also sent the courage to endure it. By herself, without His help, she would not have been able to suffer it for one day.

She knew, too, that suffering is not valuable for its own sake – God is not a sadist. The value that it can yield comes from our simple acceptance of it, and our trust in God that it is part of the great treasury of merit that He is able to use for His own loving purposes.

We may take comfort from this, as Therese did, by reminding ourselves that if we patiently suffer what God sends us, moment by moment, without projecting our pain into the future or indulging in self-pity, He will give us the means to undergo it.

As we have already seen, we can only endure our suffering today. We cannot suffer tomorrow's pains today, and there is no benefit in recalling yesterday's pain. We may trust God to give us "our daily bread" in every respect, and for those of us who are suffering physically, this includes the strength to bear the cross we have been given. This point is worth repeating, because we so often forget. There is only the present moment in which to offer our pain to God.

For us, today, the help that God gives us certainly includes pain-killers. Yet these are not without danger. We know now that it is very possible to become addicted to strong pain-killers, but as long as they are taken carefully, under the guidance of a doctor, I believe it is better to use these means for as long as we need them. Sometimes they work well, sometimes they are of little use. I take pain-killers as prescribed, and leave the outcome to God.

When we read of St Therese's extremity of pain, and the prolongation she endured without relief, a modern reader might assume she was simply a masochist, someone who enjoyed suffering, and that it did not cost her much to persevere.

This would be quite wrong. As we have seen, the young saint never once asked God for more suffering, even though she took care to make the most of that which He was already giving her.

No joy of any kind lurked in the pain itself. St Therese was not a masochistic person; she had always enjoyed life, espccially in the company of her fellow nuns and the sisters from her own family. She was known as cheerful, humorous and high spirited. Nothing in her psychology suggests that any pleasure would result from undergoing pain.

Similarly, when pain comes to us, as it surely will at some point in our lives, we are not to beg for more or seek to increase it. We are not Carmelite saints, and since the body is the temple of the Holy Spirit it is a virtue to take good care of it and not to test it beyond our endurance.

Only the knowledge that Christ can use our willing acceptance of His gift, that He is glad that we should wish to share in His sufferings on the Cross, makes our own pain bearable and even worthwhile. Without this, our pain would simply be a waste, a curse. That is indeed how other faiths see it, and those with no faith at all cannot bring any good from their own pain.

That is why the Catholic faith is so much deeper and more satisfying. It is this doctrine which brought me, and countless others, to the Church. It is a great comfort when we are enduring pain and it is the only satisfactory answer to the question of why pain exists: it exists because God can bring such great good from it, if we only cooperate with Him.

Of course, without the disobedience of our first parents, Adam and Eve, pain would not have entered the world. Because of their reckless disregard of God's commandment not to eat of the Tree of the Knowledge of Good and Evil, suffering is now part of the human condition.

But this disobedience, so wrong in itself, came about because God gave them, as He gives to us, the blessing of free will.

And the most wonderful and miraculous consequence of that first sin is that the pain and suffering it brought are now the means by which God can give us great blessings and can work miracles, as long as we co-operate with Him.

Chapter Five:

Emotional Suffering

(I) Bereavement

While physical suffering might seem the most urgent and intense form of pain, emotional suffering can be just as hard - sometimes even harder - to endure.

For physical suffering there are pain-killers and physical comforts, but although there are also medicines that help us live through emotional pain and cope with its effects, they can take longer to bring results. While immensely useful and even lifesaving, they can become addictive, and care must be taken when using them.

Later in this chapter we will look at the various means we have for dealing with emotional pain, both through medication and with different types of psychological help.

First, though, we will want to be sure our emotional pain is not a false cross.

We saw in Chapter Three that many types of emotional suffering are quite unnecessary. We may be sure that God does not want us to be unnecessarily anxious, worried, fearful or resentful. We discussed the ways in which we burden ourselves with useless mental pain, and we saw how counselling, psychiatric help and good spiritual direction can equip us with the understanding we need so that we may be free from it.

Nevertheless, while many of us never undergo severe physical suffering, we will all have to face real, emotional pain at some point in our lives.

From this cross there is no escape.

Ever since the Fall of Man we have been living in a flawed world, as flawed people. No matter how happy and prosperous our lives may be today, we cannot know how we will fare tomorrow.

The only certainty we can have in this life is that one day it will end, and we – and all those we love – will die.

Perhaps our death, and the deaths of our loved ones, will be peaceful and come painlessly at the end of a long life, well lived and leaving happy memories. Yet, however well we may think we have prepared for it, the final parting will be sad beyond anything we have known.

If you have already experienced the death of someone close to you, you will have lived through the grief that accompanies it. To those who have no faith, the anguish will be more terrible. Even though our Christian faith assures us of an afterlife, the death of a loved one is the most painful experience we will ever undergo.

We may know, with our intellect, that death is not the end; we may believe wholeheartedly that we will be reunited one day with all those we have lost. But that day seems far off, and meanwhile we have to live through the sadness, the despair, the grieving that seem endless to us who are left behind.

Even Jesus experienced this grief.

He knew He was God as well as man, and yet when his friend Lazarus died we are told that He wept.

Jesus also knew that He had the power to resurrect Lazarus, but He also understood that this event was singular, and that once He had returned to His Father in heaven, such a miracle would never be repeated.

The church tells us that one day our souls and bodies will be reunited, but it does not – cannot – tell us when this event will happen. And although we may all hope one day to meet in Heaven, this too seems shadowy and unreal when we are in the full throes of bereavement.

I recounted earlier how in my near-fatal car crash I experienced life after death, and I know now that this is a real prospect for all of us. But knowing this did not help me very much when I lost my own parents and other family members. What hurt was their absence now, the huge hole in my life that each bereavement left, the daily struggle that had to be lived through afresh each morning without the comforting knowledge that my loved one was still there.

I trained as a bereavement counsellor and have worked with many clients suffering prolonged grief. Most of them were referred through my church, and were men and women with a firm faith, yet this did not ease their experience of loss.

Grief is physical, as well as emotional.

The phrase "a heavy heart" is based on the actual, physical heaviness we feel in the area of our heart when we are grieving.

"Heartbreak", "heartache", and similar terms also describe actual physical pains we feel when suffering loss or shock.

Besides the huge loss that death inevitably brings, there are other losses, less final perhaps than death, but still painful and bitter.

We may grieve the loss of an ability, such as deafness or blindness. Many – perhaps most – older people lose some of their physical independence and have to rely on others to help them with tasks they used to do.

From my own experience I know how devastating this can be. Because of a serious car accident, I went from being a free and independent person to someone in a wheelchair; from being proud of never needing others' help to the state of always having to ask for assistance, even in relatively simple tasks.

Some of us suffer amputations or medical conditions that deprive us of our abilities.

All these are bereavements, and we should not criticise ourselves for taking as long as we need to mourn our losses.

One of my clients experienced the most profound loss he had ever known when his only son became paralysed in a road accident. Not only did he mourn for his son's present affliction, he had to grieve the loss of the person he thought his son would be. As a parent, he naturally wanted the young man to succeed in his career, to start a family and to live a long and fruitful life. Now, in a second, all those hopes were dashed, and he did not know how to come to terms with his grief.

The young man himself was mourning the loss of his own abilities, and was struggling to accept the severe limitations his new condition imposed. With long-term therapy, both physical and emotional, he did eventually regain some movement in one arm, but otherwise he was going to have to live in a restricted state, dependent on others for everything concerning his bodily needs, and unable to pursue the teaching career he had planned.

It was a cause of great sadness to both that neither had been able to find consolation in a religious faith. I suggested that the father should begin to pray each day, even though he did not think anyone would be listening. I asked him to set aside a period of half an hour in the evening, when he would spend fifteen minutes in pure grief – crying, if that was what he felt like doing - and later writing down his grieving thoughts and describing his dashed hopes.

Only fifteen minutes, I emphasized; any longer would be unproductive. The next fifteen minutes he was to spend in a state of mental quietness, perhaps meditating, perhaps sending loving thoughts to his son in hospital, and finishing with a prayer, which he could call an "aspiration" if he wished. I suggested the formula, "Lord, if you are there, please comfort and sustain us."

Later, the father began to attend a bereavement group run by laypeople, in which he could talk about his feelings and know that others would understand and support him.

These efforts helped him greatly, and although I don't know whether he ever acquired any faith in God, by the time he left therapy I knew that at least he was able to live with the knowledge that his son was alive and not in any pain.

The chief problem for this father was that, although he had indeed loved his son very much, that same love had been conditional on the young man's potential future success. When that hope was taken away, the relationship had to change for both their sakes.

When at last he came to terms with the limitations that had been imposed on his son, the father began to reach deeper within and to feel the stirring of unconditional love, the type of deep love of which Henri Nouwen has written so beautifully. Henceforth, the son was not seen as a potential achiever, to be loved for his success, but as a lovable, precious human being, the love for whom was not dependent on any success but simply for being his son.

This is the truth that all of us face when someone we love is stricken by illness or suddenly needs increased care.

It is a truth that our society prefers to ignore, that its sick and elderly citizens, those who are no longer of any apparent "use" to society, are worthy of love and respect and care, simply because they are human beings. They are certainly not useless to God, they are of infinite value and are loved with unimaginable compassion, just as we ourselves are.

This contempt for the elderly, weak and disabled among us is a manifestation of the great demon Mammon, which sees people as valuable only when they can work and produce goods for our consumption.

We Christians know that God loves us regardless of our "productivity"; that He does not make any conditions upon us except that of accepting His love in the face of our own unworthiness. As the Bible tells us, nothing can separate us from that love, not even our own apparently unlovable natures.

If we reach our rock bottom, as alcoholics say, we can all the more readily reach out to the only One who heals us, the only One in whom we can place our complete trust.

In that state, we know that one day all our bereavements will be healed, that everyone we have lost will be restored to us and that which is broken will be made whole again. Not in this life, of course, but in the next – that is the hope all Christians have because of the One who suffered and died that we might come to know this great truth.

Encouragingly, I have been privileged to know a number of people who, limited by their dependent bodies to a life in a wheelchair, nevertheless enjoy happy and fulfilled lives. Some have found new work in writing, as I have done.

One elderly man in particular, who lived in Jerusalem, was bed-ridden and completely dependent on his family and carers to keep him alive, was truly an inspiration.

Before a progressive illness reduced his physical state, he had been a well-known professor of philosopher at a prestigious university. After he had become ill, he was still respected for his work, which consisted of writing a series of books that continue to give spiritual encouragement and consolation to others in similar situations who feel their lives are useless after such a blow.

In his former career he taught thousands of students and inspired them to succeed in their own careers. Later, in his physically disabled state, he reached hundreds of thousands of people, from all walks of life, who still find great meaning and inspiration in his books.

Similar problems may be faced when parents discover their children are ill, or have been born with a genetic problem such as Down Syndrome.

Such children will, like the young man described above, never be able to fulfil their parents' wishes for them, especially if those parents had been high achievers and valued people for their apparent success in life.

A Down Syndrome child is not going to become a leading scientist, a lawyer or a professor. But he or she is a human being who needs love and care, and it is quite possible that this child was sent by God to these particular families so that they might all grow in love, compassion and spiritual understanding.

There have been many cases of young children who have suffered from a debilitating disease and who knew they were going to die, but who have been able not only to accept this situation but to inspire and comfort their own parents. Children are closer to God than are many adults, and can receive and pass on to others the love and strength they draw from Him.

The loss of a child is perhaps the very worst loss that can happen to us. It seems so wrong, so unnatural. We expect our children to outlive us, and when this does not happen it is tremendously hard to accept.

There is a Jewish story – a true tale – of a Hasidic family whose father was a revered rabbi and whose wife was also a very spiritual person.

While the rabbi was away on a journey, the couple's two sons contracted a fatal illness and died.

The wife did not know how to break the news to her husband. The two children had been their pride and joy, and they loved them both profoundly, especially since they themselves were middle-aged and the wife was past childbearing.

After much prayer, when the husband returned his wife said to him, "If we were asked to look after a valuable jewel, would the owner have the right to ask for it back one day?"

"Of course," the rabbi said, thinking she was outlining a legal case.

But she went on, "The Lord entrusted us with two most precious jewels, and now He has come to take them back."

Then the rabbi understood, and although their grief was heavy, it was because the couple were close to God that they were eventually able to accept their terrible loss. They knew God would take care of His "jewels" and that one day they would all be reunited in the world to come.

If you are suffering from bereavement as you read this, I hope you will one day draw closer to God through this painful loss. Like many before you, you may find you need help in accepting your situation. If so, please do seek out a counsellor qualified in bereavement counselling. He or she will listen to you and will understand how you feel. A bereavement group may be helpful to you, as those who have been newly bereaved can feel isolated, as though nobody wants to listen to them or be around them at this time.

If you are a Christian, you know that eventually all will be well and that your loved ones are "not lost, but gone before", as is written on so many gravestones. Even so, you can't carry out a "spiritual bypass". You may know the truth intellectually, but emotionally it still cuts deep and each day, each moment, may feel like an insurmountable hurdle to be overcome so that you can continue without the presence of the person you love.

You may be familiar with the five stages of grieving, as outlined by Elizabeth Kubler-Ross. In fact, to call them "stages" is a little misleading, as they usually don't follow a logical pattern. You may feel any one of them at any time after bereavement, and it's helpful to know what they are so that you may situate yourself in this respect, knowing that all these phases are perfectly normal.

They are: denial, anger, bargaining, depression and acceptance.

Although this seems like a linear progression – and for some people, that is exactly how they are experienced – they are simply names given to the feelings that crop up at any stage during a grieving process.

Normally, that process takes about two years in the case of a major bereavement, and during that time you may feel any of those stages, and may even undergo more than one at the same time. Each person's grieving is unique.

The phase of anger means exactly that; anger with the person who has died, or anger at the deprivation of something important to you. Because we never like to speak ill of the dead, mourners sometimes suppress this perfectly normal feeling, and it then goes underground to fester as resentment or depression. If you experience anger in this way, and there is no one around you to whom you may freely express it, you can pour out your feelings to a priest or a grief counsellor, knowing they will understand and not judge you for it.

Remember, too, that anger need not be against an individual. You might feel angry at a disease or a set of circumstances; many alcoholics and addicts feel angry at the disease of addiction, and this is a healthy response.

Denial may crop up at any time during a bereavement. We can temporarily forget what has happened, or try to disbelieve it

– we may tell ourselves that the hospital made a mistake, or that it must apply to someone else. An often-reported effect of denial is that we may find ourselves lifting the phone to speak to the deceased person, or suddenly realise that we are driving over to the home of someone who died, momentarily forgetting that they are no longer there.

Bargaining is another form of denial. Often it accompanies a medical warning or diagnosis, when we try to convince ourselves that a certain outcome is not inevitable. An alcoholic may try to cut down on drinking and limit her intake to two glasses of wine a day, in the hope that in doing so she may find she is not really an alcoholic, after all. We may seek a second medical opinion, or a third. If the problem is real, however, such efforts are doomed to failure.

Depression can also prevail at any time. Sadness at the loss of a person or a situation is absolutely normal, and, like anger, should not be repressed. Here, counselling is extremely helpful, and a skilled therapist will be able to help his client endure the sadness and see whether other feelings are being masked by the depression. Often, unexpressed anger will be found to cause a depression. Sometimes, the sadness is simply the huge loss of someone or something we love, and the recognition that we may never see them again.

Depression can be life-threatening if it goes on too long, and medical help must be sought if it seems overwhelming. There's no shame in taking medication to help you through a very difficult time and help you recover from the grief you feel.

The stage of acceptance is a bitter-sweet feeling. We accept our loss, acknowledging the hard truth that someone or something has gone for ever, and that we cannot turn back the clock. We do not try to soften the blow, but neither do we magnify or dwell on it. Nothing will be the same, but life goes on, and we realize
that we can, after all, live with the loss without being emotionally handicapped by it.

Sometimes people feel ashamed of accepting the loss. It can seem as though acceptance means forgetting the person or situation and thus losing them forever. It is not really like that, of course. Our good memories will never disappear, and we can be thankful for the happy and fulfilled times we have had, while also acknowledging that they are now in the past.

There is no set time for a grieving process to last. Sometimes, especially if someone we love has been battling a long illness, we may actually have worked through some of our grief before their death. If the illness has been painful and difficult we might feel relieved that the patient no longer suffers. But even when this is true, grieving can go on longer than we expect.

If, after two years, the emotions of grief are still so strong that they interfere with normal living, it's wise to seek the help of a counsellor and a doctor. It's important to choose someone specialised in bereavement counselling, who will know how to help you through the maze of mixed feelings these different phases can create.

What is *not* helpful is trying to avoid or suppress any of these feelings. In Western societies death is a subject most people try to deny. The many attempts at superficial rejuvenation and the denial of the effects of time are the results of living in a society without a religious faith.

If people believe this life is all we have, and that death means annihilation, it's not surprising that they will try to postpone death for as long as possible and refuse to accept their own and others' ageing. For this reason, I believe efforts to mask the effects of time – plastic surgery, botox, and so on – are truly harmful to the spirit. They are a denial of the reality that our physical lives on Earth are only the first stage in our existence, and that after death we are not eliminated but are taken into the next stage.

We Catholics are very fortunate in having a faith that

reassures us of our continued existence after death. That is a blessing we share with other Christians, Orthodox Jews, and Muslims.

Unlike Hindus or Buddhists, we do not have to contemplate an endless, dreary cycle of karmic suffering in punishing circumstances.

Furthermore, we Christians know that Jesus Christ has paid the price for our many sins, and while Catholics believe we may need further purification in Purgatory, we have the certainty that as long as we die at peace with God, we shall ultimately enter into Heaven.

I can personally vouch for the fact that death is not the end of our journey, but the beginning of another, greater, life. Through my own Near Death Experience, I have the complete assurance that when my physical body dies, my soul will be free to carry on its journey to the next life. I encourage everyone to read about the many Near Death Experiences that have been documented, as they will strengthen your religious faith and can bring about a spiritual upliftment that no amount of plastic surgery could match.

*   *   *

St Therese was introduced to bereavement very early in her life. We saw in Chapter One how deeply she was affected by her mother's untimely death. She went with her father and older sisters to live in Lisieux, but although the family tried their best to compensate for this great loss, Therese gradually had to let go of three of her sisters as they entered convents one by one and left her behind.

In the end, only Therese, her sister Celine, and their father were left at home in Lisieux, and after Therese herself had become a novice in the Lisieux Carmel only Celine and their father remained outside.

And even worse was to come, because their father, Louis, developed signs of mental illness, probably dementia, and ultimately was forced to live in a care home for his own safety.

The spectacle of Therese's once so wise and loving father having been reduced to a state of helplessness caused her tremendous grief. Added to the normal grieving process was the stigma that mental illness then carried. Therese was spared nothing of the full experience of bereavement in her short life, even to the point of losing her spiritual consolations in her final eighteen months.

In Chapter Two we saw what effect this great trial had upon the soon-to-be saint. Undergoing what we call the Dark Night of the Soul was a terrible experience, but Therese did not allow her soul to become submerged by this great bereavement. She continued to practice her faith in every way she could, but in that final year she says that she derived no consolation from it. No longer did she experience the closeness of God; she simply continued to pray and to follow the Rule of Carmel as much as her illness allowed, and did not confide to anyone what was happening to her.

We know that all her consolations came back to her as she lay dying, because her face in the last moments was lit by joy and even ecstasy. She had carried her burden unseen and unrelieved during that last year of her life, and in doing so had shown tremendous courage and endurance.

What I take from this is that, no matter what my circumstances may be, even if my path is through the Dark Night of the Soul, I do not have to surrender my faith.

We know that Jesus suffered on the Cross, and that St Therese willingly endured her own earthly suffering in imitation of Him. There is literally no bereavement we may experience that He and our saints have not undergone.

In our suffering, we are not alone.

It can become a chariot to lift us up so that we become closer to God.

Chapter Six

Emotional sufferings

(II) Suffering caused by others

Not all serious suffering is due to a bereavement. There are many other forms of mental suffering we may experience in this life.

Other people may cause us much undeserved unhappiness. We may suffer because our spouse has betrayed us and left us for another. Our friends may prove false when we are going through a trial. We may lose our job because of lies spread about us, or unjust accusations, or simple economic circumstances that force the closure of a business.

Someone we love may cause us great anguish because they turn to drugs or alcohol, and their life spirals out of control. Perhaps we have tried to help someone in desperate circumstances, but to no avail. We have to witness many injustices in our daily life, some great – such as the unjust distribution of wealth in our society – and some lesser, perhaps when we are blamed for something we did not do.

All these sufferings have two things in common: they are unavoidable, and they are very painful.

To talk of offering these sufferings to Christ may seem to give little comfort. In the case of physical pain, we know that He endured a terrible death on the cross, for our sake, and we know from this that any physical pain we may be suffering is something that He, too, has borne. When we offer our own physical pains to Him we can unite them with those He suffered on the cross, precisely because we know that they correspond to His own suffering.

How can this be true of emotional pain? Has Christ suffered like us, in His emotions? Will He understand our own suffering from the inside out, as it were, because He has also gone through the same experience?

In the case of death, we have seen that He did indeed suffer. He knew that He could, and would, bring Lazarus back to life after death. But he also knew that everyone else would have to suffer the physical death that Lazarus did, and that Lazarus's own death was not avoided but merely postponed. He knew, too, that He Himself was going to experience physical death and mental anguish on the cross.

He must have grieved for all of us, in those dreadful hours of His crucifixion. He would have foreseen all the great trials that human beings would have to undergo, far into the future.

He knew the desperate pain we would have to go through in circumstances that we did not create and cannot control. As we have just seen, He knew how terrible it is to lose someone to death, and that there could be no short cuts through our grieving. In that instant, when we are told that He wept for His friend, He surely thought of us too, His church, and of all those with no faith who would have no sense of consolation in a future heaven.

As well as the deep grief of loss, Jesus suffered in many other ways during His life on Earth.

One of the worst forms of suffering is betrayal, and He knew the full force of this suffering as He undertook His redemptive mission. At the Last Supper, Judas betrayed His Lord, and Jesus knew beforehand that he would do so. What a terrible sadness this must have caused Him – that among His chosen band of disciples was one who would sell Him to the enemy for a paltry bag of cash.

Not only Judas, but Peter, the very disciple on whom Jesus would found His church, betrayed Him during the time of Jesus' trial. Again, Jesus knew this would happen and even warned

Peter of this danger, but Peter completely lost his head through fear and three times denied being a follower of Jesus.

Abandonment by His closest followers as well as by the crowd that gathered outside Pilate's courthouse must have cut Jesus to the quick. He forgave them all, but as a human being He suffered just as we all do when someone we love betrays and abandons us. Jesus did not resort to a "spiritual bypass". He felt all the sadness, all the loss, that everyone feels when someone trusted lets us down.

Jesus suffered outright rejection on numerous occasions during His ministry. Beginning with the rejection by His neighbours and acquaintances when He first proclaimed the Kingdom of God, He was continually rejected by the "experts" in religious faith, the Pharisees, those doctors of the law whose name has become a byword for incomprehension and for hypocrisy.

The Pharisees knew the Bible backwards and forwards and had studied every word of it, and to us, their rejection of the Lord is perplexing. We Christians can see so many clues in the Old Testament that Jesus is indeed the Messiah that we wonder how anyone could have missed this point while Jesus was alive, and was performing the miracles of healing and understanding that testified to His identity.

Yet, even today, the majority of the world still rejects Jesus. Some have been raised in another religion and find it impossible to consider Jesus's claims with any sort of objectivity. Some – especially today, if they live among militant Islamists – face certain death if they declare themselves to be Christians. Despite this, many courageous men and women do convert to Christianity and openly identify themselves as such; their brave conduct should shame those of us in the West who take our freedom of religion for granted, and yet still hesitate to say we are Christians.

The persecution of Christians today echoes the sufferings of

Jesus Himself during His Passion. The whipping, the scourging, the crowning with thorns and the terrible indignity of the crucifixion testify to the hatred of God which motivated the authorities of His day – and which motivates the enemies of Judaism and Christianity even today.

The devil will go to any lengths to frustrate the Will of God and prevent the return of Jesus, the Messiah. He tried hard to interfere in the events of Jesus's life, little realising that in fact the suffering he caused then only gave even greater power to the forces of truth and goodness from Heaven, leading not to disgrace and ultimate annihilation but to joy and eternal life.

Today, we see how the devil uses anything and anyone he can muster in the cause of preventing Jesus' Second Coming. He strives through terrorists, atheists, lukewarm agnostics, and all those addicted to sin, to persuade the world to abandon Jesus and His mission.

We see this battle played out fully in the fate of Jerusalem, which today remains the physical location where Jesus will one day return. If a force opposed to Christianity can gain permanent control of this vital area, so the devil reasons, then Jesus will not be able to return there, and His followers will abandon Him once again.

The world persecutes the Jews because they are Jesus's blood family. It tries to oust them from their hard-won homeland, the portion of the world which God has given to them in perpetuity, so that Jesus will find nobody and nowhere to welcome Him when He comes back.

The devil tries similar tactics with all Christians at some time during our lives. He besets us with thoughts of annihilation, of nothingness, that our faith is futile. He tempts us with sinful thoughts so that we too may abandon God and pursue our own most tempting addictions. Jesus knows what we endure, and He will strengthen us when we turn to Him, but He always allows us our free choice; God never forces anyone to act or to believe in a certain way.

If we continually give in to sin, and never repent, we will finally be separated from God, and this is the most painful form of suffering that is possible for a human being to endure.

It is this final pain which Jesus endured for us, and it is the worst of all – the separation from God which He experienced on the cross as He bore the weight of the world's sins on His shoulders. He cried out His feeling of abandonment – that God had forsaken Him – in His last moments; but beyond this agony lay the acceptance that His mission was now accomplished in full.

He told us this when he declared, "It is finished", and then yielded His spirit to the Father's hands. The worst had happened and it had not defeated Him; He was victorious, and He left us with this final hope and consolation.

After His death, He appeared to His disciples to reassure them that all was well. As God, He knew the story ended with victory, not the apparent defeat that the world saw. But that knowledge did not spare Him the terrible trial of suffering that had to precede that victory; and we will find it so in our own lives.

The problem is that when we are consumed by grief, in the midst of desolation, it is very, very hard to raise our thoughts to Christ. We do well to practice it in the everyday circumstances of life, in happiness as well as sadness, in every task we undertake and every pain we feel, from a minor nuisance to a major problem. If we have formed this habit in better times, then when we are truly grief-stricken we will be able to recall it and to remember that this is what we are asked to do.

Making a daily morning offering is vital to all Catholics. Many make the first
prayer of the day an offering to the Sacred Heart, accepting in advance all the troubles that may arise that day and offering

them to Jesus in union with His holy sacrifice in the Mass.

At the back of this book you will find an Appendix, giving suggestions for how to make a morning offering as well as how to begin daily meditation. If we can persist in these forms of prayer during happy or uneventful periods, we can rely on them to help us through the difficult patches. We will know, deep down, that all is well, despite the trials we may undergo.

The rosary can bring great consolation in times of trouble, as well being a joyful link with Our Lady throughout our busy lives.

When children feel secure in their mother's love, they naturally turn to her constantly for advice, help and comfort. They bring her all their daily happenings, knowing she will understand and support them. If they have enjoyed playing with their friends that day, or have received praise from a teacher, they tell their mother, knowing that she will be just as pleased as they are, and their happiness is increased because of this sharing.

In the same way, children bring their problems to their mothers, finding relief simply in telling her about them. Perhaps someone has spoken harshly to them, or they have been unjustly punished at school; maybe another child spread false rumours about them, or insulted them.

They know that, whatever it may be, their mother will help them to face each trial and will intervene on their behalf when a real wrong has been done to them.

A good mother is never neutral, she is always concerned with the physical and mental state of her child, and will offer comfort and understanding in all the circumstances of their lives.

Our Lady, the most perfect mother who ever lived and who is also our own spiritual mother, will always listen to us whenever we seek her company. When help is called for, she will be there. When all we need is someone to hear our problems, to really listen to us, she is ready.

We may pray to her in any form of words we like, but she herself has asked us to pray the rosary, and whenever we do so we know that she is listening and is pleased with our prayer.

If we pray the rosary with the attention it deserves, recalling the events of each mystery as we recite our Hail Mary, we will find the scenes of the Bible unfolding before us as we speak. We will share in Mary's joys and sorrows, in her exaltation and in her final triumph, and we will draw closer to her, and further from our own daily troubles, as we do so.

Saint Padre Pio, the great modern stigmatist and spiritual advisor, suffered greatly throughout his life from all the emotional problems I have described above. He was mistrusted, abandoned, rejected and disliked by many in the church who failed to understand him. He suffered the pain of the stigmata, and was sometimes reviled as a fake, a phoney, when he was in the midst of battling against the devil on behalf of his spiritual children.

To this saint, the rosary was a tremendous daily comfort. He formed the habit of praying the rosary wherever he was, in whatever conditions. He always carried a rosary and would recite the prayers as he walked from his cell to the church, and back again. After his death, his reputation as a truly saintly priest grew stronger every year until his sanctity was finally recognized and he was canonised on June 16th, 2002.

Because St Pio knows, as does Our Lord, what it is like to be rejected and betrayed by people we should be able to trust, this mighty saint will hear our prayers for help and assist us in persevering with the right course of action. He will help us to strengthen our devotion to Jesus and Mary, and will encourage us when we become weary.

Accepting insults and perjuries, without demanding

reparation, is a way in which we can imitate Christ. We all know the instructions the Lord gives us, to return good for evil, to refuse to take part in aggression, to disarm the enemy with prayer rather than returning insult for insult.

Great saints have always known this, and have willingly followed the path which Sufis, the mystics of Islam, call "The Way of Blame". The purpose of this path is simple: it works to neutralise hatred in the world, and to subdue pride in the heart of the would-be saint. Nobody, before Jesus, had taught this path, because it is so difficult and seems to lead nowhere. But then, carrying our cross makes no sense to anyone who is not a Christian.

We know – from personal experience, from the words of Jesus, and the writings of the saints – that suffering is the path to sainthood. And we know, too, that we are called to be saints. This is why the Way of Blame can be a real way to reach that noble state, because the suffering we willingly undergo without retaliation humbles us to become more like Jesus.

The Sufi mystics also value this path as a means to self-abasement before God.

I have found no trace of it anywhere before Jesus Himself taught it, but we know that the Sufis value Christianity and the teachings of Jesus, whom they regard as a prophet. It seems clear that they drew the principles of the Way of Blame from their study of Scripture, and it is a path that various Sufi Sheiks have taught their followers.

It is easy to write about this path, but almost impossible to follow in real life, until we understand the value of suffering.

We can all think of examples of where we have been mistreated and falsely accused. It is natural to want to clear our names, and if we have been insulted in our professional capacity it may be necessary to do so, so that we may continue to work.

But there are also many occasions in our personal lives where this situation can arise.

One of the times my husband and I experienced this form of suffering was when, as students, we were falsely accused by a landlord of breaking tiles at the house we were renting. The tiles had in fact broken when we first lit a fire in the ancient fireplace. The tiling expert who was called to replace them said it was a wonder they had not cracked long before, and he proceeded to put in identical new tiles so that no harm was done to the property.

Yet the false accusation was deeply hurtful, and we puzzled over why the Lord had allowed it to happen. We concluded that it was, indeed, the Way of Blame that had been offered to us as a sacrifice we could make for Him, and in a very practical way it also showed us what it was like to be falsely accused, as Jesus had been throughout his life.

We should not mistake the Way of Blame and of non-violence for a coward's way out of a situation. It is anything but. It calls on us to master our own animal instinct for retaliation, and to be willing to be seen as offenders if necessary. It took us many months before we were able to see the truth of the situation and to offer thanks to the Lord for it. We could not avoid facing the anger and sorrow that our landlord had caused us.

We have to "feel our feelings", to experience them in all their discomfort and pain, before we can sincerely accept that suffering and offer it to Jesus.

Some people, aware of this path, try to walk it before they are ready. They blithely offer forgiveness at once when someone has hurt them, and deny that they feel angry or hurt. If we attempt to do this, however, we will only experience those feelings all the more strongly at some point. They will have to be undergone, lived through, before real forgiveness and healing can take place.

Trying to avoid the acknowledgement of suffering is quite common. Because the sad and angry feelings are so difficult to bear, and because they seem so un-Christian, some sufferers repress their anger and eventually fall prey to depression

Sometimes a suffering person may seem, on the surface, to be happy and jovial. There is something about them, however, that friends and family – and certainly an experienced counsellor – will sense; that the happy smile begins to feel forced, and underneath lies a heap of painful emotions that the sufferer has repressed, perhaps for years. In the end, they may erupt into physical or verbal violence, which shocks all those around them because it apparently arises quite out of the blue.

Repression is harmful. It stops people from seeking help when they most need it, and it causes hidden anger to "come out sideways", as it were, so that innocent people become its victims.

This is another case where counselling can help. If we have buried our painful feelings so deeply that we do not know they are there, and yet find ourselves unaccountably depressed or angry, a skilled counsellor can lead us through this experience and bring us safely to a place where healing and understanding can take place. Only then are we able to let this suffering ascend to Christ, who will transform it into valuable merit for the work of His church throughout the world.

Before we end this chapter, I want to look at another, very common, form of suffering caused by others, which is unavoidable and can only be borne through faith and trust in the Lord.

This suffering is the anguish our loved ones may cause us when they are addicted to drugs or alcohol, or are being abused or harmed by another person.

In some cases we can offer practical help. We can offer to pay for treatment, if our means allow, we can support them with our love and perhaps offer them a refuge in our home, if they need it, and we can offer financial support – again, if we are able.

But addictions are notoriously difficult to cure. The organizations of AA, NA, and other Twelve-Step programmes do offer real hope to the suffering addict, and it's my firm belief that they work because people following them learn to put their trust in God, however they may describe Him.

Rehab centres are very helpful, especially in short-term detoxing and encouraging the addict to take the first steps towards living a normal life, but for the long-term well-being and recovery of the addict, a Twelve-Step programme has no equal.

The problem is that the family members, friends or spouses of the addict feel their loved one's pain so deeply and yet are powerless to cure them.

We have to accept that we ourselves really are powerless over other people. And this is difficult to take on board, particularly if the addict is a spouse or a child. In the past, we have been able to nurture this person with our love and support them in their hardships. Faced with a serious addiction, however, we can do very little.

There are Twelve-Step programmes, such as Alanon, for family members troubled by the addiction or alcoholism of someone they love. They are extremely effective in allowing the sufferer to take a step back from the distressing situation and to "let go and let God", as the saying goes.

We have to accept that we are not God, and that only God, working through the programmes and in the form of helpful and compassionate counsellors, can help the addict to recover.

Because other people may well know of the drug addiction or alcoholism – or other serious addiction – there is a lot of shame attached to dealing with these problems. Nobody wants to admit that their beloved son or daughter, husband or wife, suffers from addiction. Some family members refuse to attend Alanon meetings, which are focused on how to live with the problem, because "somebody might find out about it".

This is a harmful attitude. It is based on a common fear – that meetings like this can lead to gossip, and that gossip would be harmful to the family and the addict. In fact, everyone at such a meeting is facing the same problems, and nobody is likely to gossip about it. Moreover, nobody has to give their real name at these meetings. You can call yourself by any name you like, and your problems will be kept confidential.

It can be very hard to speak at these meetings, especially at the first meeting you attend. But if you persevere, you will find people with very similar problems who will give you wholehearted support and encouragement as you walk this path.

To be willing to talk about these subjects with others can be part of our own healing. It will – to some extent – give us a taste of the Way of Blame, because we have to have the humility to acknowledge that something is very wrong in our own family, and that we need help to deal with it.

If anyone reading this is beset by similar doubts, I strongly encourage you to give a Twelve-Step group your best try. It may be your best hope to save the life of someone you love. You do have to humble yourself to talk about it, but this will be part of your own healing, as you learn to surrender the misunderstanding that you can heal the person you love. Only God can do that, and participating in groups like these will allow you to let God into your life and into the life of the person you love, to bring about ultimate healing.

Here is a practical hint for dealing with this pain on a daily basis: when a thought or mental picture of the addicted person comes to mind, see it as God's reminder to pray for him or her. Visualise that person surrounded by the light and love of God, and gently turn them over to the care of that loving God. Then let go yourself. Realize that you are not God, and you can do no more. But He can, and He will.

*   *   *

St Therese can be our model for facing these difficulties, too. She accepted the many trials of her Carmelite way without making any complaint. Sometimes she was fed what were literally scraps of food – the kitchen's leftovers – because she ate them without grumbling, and the other nuns simply assumed she enjoyed such disgusting meals.

Sometimes, especially during the early stages of her illness, the freezing temperatures endured by the sisters caused Therese real suffering. Only as the full extent of her disease became known was she told by the Prioress that she must accept some mitigation of the Rule, and Therese accepted this only because she did so under obedience.

For herself, she never sought any lightening of the daily burden, even when in pain and growing weaker. She took every chance to mortify her body, because she knew that this type of suffering was very valuable in saving souls, and for the sake of Jesus she persisted in following this – to us – utterly foolish way of life.

There was, however, another great trial ahead.

All the sisters had loved their father very much, especially because he was their sole parent after the death of their mother. Louis Martin was the model of a fervent Catholic father, and taught his daughters thoroughly from an early age in the way of living that was most acceptable to God: daily Mass, frequent confession, bearing burdens cheerfully, giving to the poor, and never putting oneself forward for any special privilege.

All were very proud of this dignified, serene older man, and enjoyed the attention others gave him as they walked to and from Mass, or enjoyed quiet country walks and recreation.

So high was the esteem in which he was held by his family and all those who knew him that his swift decline into mental illness left them aghast.

In our day, the taboo against mentioning mental illness is finally being lifted. Even so, many feel ashamed of admitting that they or a family member is suffering in this way. It is almost as though they fear being blamed for the illness, as though in some way it could have been avoided had they or their loved one only behaved better, showed more understanding, or – especially in Northern European peoples – cultivated a more stoical attitude to life.

A hundred years ago, however, the taboo was so firmly entrenched that mental illness was literally unmentionable. If you had to talk about it, if you or someone you loved suffered in this way, you referred to it only in hushed tones, if at all. The shame people felt in connection with it was overwhelming.

Even in the Carmelite convent, where the sisters might have been expected to show more tolerance and understanding, the taboo was still strong. Saints in the making, they were nevertheless children of their time, a time when mental illness was very little understood and carried enormous stigma.

Such was the situation that St. Therese and her family found themselves in when the kind, wise and intelligent father they had known and loved all their lives began to show signs of dementia.

In early childhood, St.Therese had undergone a painful vision whilst at home, in the garden of Les Buissonets. She had seen a figure passing by at the end of the garden, a strange and disquieting person who looked like her father but whose head seemed to be covered by a cloth. She could make no sense of it, but when, many years later, Louis Martin started to speak and act in unfamiliar, illogical ways, she recalled the early vision and wondered whether it had been a presentiment.

As the elderly man's illness grew worse he could no longer be cared for at home, and needed to enter a mental hospital. No longer could his deteriorating state be denied and covered up; it was only too plain for all to see.

Some blamed the Martin sisters for "deserting" their father to enter Carmel, even though Louis Martin had given his full consent. As we have seen, the need to blame someone was very strong in those days, and it is still common today.

The pain which the decline of their beloved parent caused to the sisters was immense. On one of the last occasions when they could speak with him at all, he pointed with his finger towards the sky, and uttered "au ciel" (in heaven). To Therese and her sisters, it was as though he was bidding an earthly farewell to them, in a last flash of lucidity, and reassuring them that they would all meet in heaven.

It was heartbreaking, and made all the more difficult because they were unable to talk about their father's illness with anyone outside their family.

Today, there are support groups for those with family members suffering from dementia. Day care centres help alleviate the daily strain of living with this terrible illness, but if the sufferer lives long enough, they will inevitably have to have either 24-hour nursing care at home or end their days in a nursing home.

The former solution is very expensive and out of the question for most families. A nursing home can be a suitable setting for a dementia patient, but good ones are very thin on the ground, and again, finances come into play. If people have medical insurance, a comfortable place may be available in a good home that takes real care with their patients; if not, it is often a lottery as to what the family can afford, and what the government will pay for.

The Martins were comparatively wealthy and money was not a problem for them, so at least St Therese and her sisters were spared this hardship. Nevertheless, since understanding of the illness was so little advanced, many homes failed to take the best care of dementia sufferers.

To this shame and distress of the illness was added the helplessness of the family to alleviate their father's suffering themselves, and the anxiety of how he was being treated in the home which eventually took him in.

Just as they did, we too may have to face this problem some day, and for us too the anxiety may be very great.

It is then that we will need to turn to Jesus and to Mary for help.

As with the alcoholic or addict, we are powerless to prevent the illness of dementia from taking hold in our families. At the same time, we know that prayer is the greatest help and comfort we can offer, both to the patient and in respect of our own suffering.

Here, as we have seen with earlier suffering, we will find that establishing a regular prayer routine will be an enormous benefit. If we are used to offering all our sufferings to Christ, to be united with His suffering on the cross, we will find it easier to include this mental suffering so that He may take it and transform it.

When we do this, we trust Him to take care of the person we love, and we send them the highest form of sacrifice we can offer, so that they may benefit from the healing and comforting of Jesus.

We find relief when we resign ourselves to accepting His

Will for us, in the form of this unlooked-for and deeply painful suffering. Most of us find it harder to bear the fact that someone we love is in pain, than to accept our own pain. Indeed, to us it is impossible. Thank God, therefore, that He has prepared a path for us to follow, little as we wish to do so.

I have found that in situations like these, where others are suffering and where we are powerless, special prayers are very effective. I am thinking here of Novenas, Rosaries and Mass Offerings, all of which are real currency in the treasure-house of the Lord. Although there is little we can do for the sufferer on earth, and although we ourselves may experience the depths of despair when our family members suffer, the economy of Heaven provides us with enormous resources.

It seems to me that many people with dementia are undergoing part of their purgatory before they die. After death, it is entirely possible that they may be ready for Heaven. That, surely, is a comforting thought.

Chapter Seven

Spiritual Sufferings

So far we have considered several different types of suffering, all of them painful and difficult, yet all offering a possibility of transformation when accepted and offered to God.

We have looked at the way in which Jesus, in His life on earth, suffered all the sorrows we have written about – physical and mental pain, abandonment, grief and profound sadness because of the way He knew we would also have to suffer.

|Knowing that Jesus went through so many forms of suffering Himself gives us hope. It means that He understands us, completely. It shows us that we can find understanding and loving consolation by offering our sufferings to Him, to be united with His own on the cross.

This knowledge is a priceless treasure of the Catholic church. It tells us that no matter how small or how great our own suffering may be, if we accept it willingly as coming from His hand, and as a tiny share in His own cross, He will use our love and our acceptance to help save souls and comfort others.

There is a further type of suffering which may offer the greatest potential for our own spiritual growth as well as a great opportunity to share in the Lord's cross: I am talking about spiritual suffering.

Spiritual suffering is also transformative, if we offer it to the Lord. In fact, it may be the strongest and quickest way to sainthood for many of us. It may come to us through Dark Nights of the Soul and Senses; through knowledge of our own deficiencies; and through acknowledgement of our sinful nature which has caused so much pain.

Yet, there is a difference between this and the types of suffering we have already considered.

We suffer spiritually when we see our own shortcomings, how we have failed God and failed others, and as sinners have caused great grief to Jesus and His Mother.

Jesus, however, never suffered remorse, because He never committed a sin.

As the Son of God, he was already perfect. He was tempted in all ways like ourselves, as St Paul tells us, yet He resisted them all and never sinned.

In previous chapters we have seen how Jesus's own experience of pain and sorrow enables Him to enter into our own situations, and to transform them with His love into priceless jewels. As we know, this transformation is possible only when we patiently accept everything we suffer, and offer our patience and love to Him, and only the Catholic Church teaches us about this miracle.

To other faiths, suffering is useless, but to us, it is the key to our own eventual perfection and the redemption of the world. How wonderful that God has created this divine economy which allows His sinful creatures to contribute to His own work in transforming and redeeming all that He has created!

Part of our consolation when we make this offering comes from knowing that Our Lord has Himself undergone the pain we now experience. He understands it from within, as it were; it is not strange to Him; He did not have to undergo it, but He chose to do so, for our sake. Knowing this, we take great comfort that the One who made us knows our trials and has experienced them Himself.

Sin, however, is alien to His divine nature. It is so utterly different from His own perfection that it cannot come into His presence. How, then, can He possibly understand our own predicament – we, who sin so often in our thoughts, words and deeds, in what we have done and in what we have failed to do, as the prayer says?

The answer lies in the boundless compassion of His Sacred Heart and in the whole gamut of suffering He willingly experienced in the Garden of Gethsemane and on the Cross.

Because He willed to undergo all the pain the human race can experience, He also bore the weight of guilt. As Dietrich Bonhoeffer says, Jesus did not wish to be the only person who had never felt guilt. Even though innocence was His natural state, He allowed Himself to be condemned and to experience the full horror of sin and guilt which humanity bears.

And ultimately, Bonhoeffer points out, "in His love for real human beings, Jesus becomes the one burdened by guilt – indeed, the one upon whom all human guilt ultimately falls, and the one who does not turn it away but bears it humbly and in eternal love".

Yes, in Himself, Jesus is free of all taint of sin. Yet, having lived on Earth as a man amongst us, He willingly undertook to be tempted in the wilderness. And, knowing how powerful the devil can be in tempting us human beings, Jesus understands us when we fail. He knows how fatally easy it can be to succumb to a moment's evil impulse, how strong temptations can be, for Satan knows the weaknesses of each one of us and tempts us just at our weakest spot.

Out of the limitless love He bears us, His Sacred Heart is deeply touched when we realise that we have sinned and that we are sorry. Out of our own guilt and remorse we reach towards Him in sorrow for having offended Him, and – like the father of the Prodigal Son – Jesus, so to speak, runs towards us, engulfs us in His love, and washes us clean.

Jesus of His own volition chose to leave His state as the one without sin, and on the cross He entered into the guilt of humanity. He took all our sins, all our filth, all our darkness, upon Himself. Therefore, we can be sure that although He deserved no guilt, He knows how it feels to be remorseful and contrite, and because life in such a state is unbearable, He bore it all away for us, taking it upon Himself, as the ancient scapegoat once did.

We can be sure that when, truly penitent, we confess our sins in the sacrament of reconciliation, we are absolved and forgiven. We make a new beginning, going out into the world cleansed and with a firm resolve not to sin in the future.

Being sinful creatures, we also know that it is all too likely we will soon sin again, if not in the same way, then in some new failing that causes us to stumble.

When we feel remorse of conscience (which in itself is a great gift from God), we realize how very different we are from Him. Other forms of suffering have been experienced by Jesus, and when we are feeling pain or grief, we are comforted in knowing that in this we are like Him. He went through it first, and we are akin to our God when we suffer.

Remorse highlights sharply the huge difference between ourselves and our God. As we have seen, in Him there is no sin. He never committed a single one, because He is perfection itself, whereas for us, sin is like a sharp black line drawn around our soul, cutting it off from the presence of God.

Nothing sinful can stand the light and love of God. They cannot exist together. As St John tells us, the light shines in the darkness, and the darkness cannot overcome it, for they are complete opposites. They cannot possibly be reconciled.

When we are contrite, when we are ashamed of our behaviour, we feel our own nothingness. Worse, we are actually less than nothing when we are in a state of sin, because we cannot draw close to God. Forever that division – that enormous gulf – demarcates the difference between our Creator and ourselves, His creatures. Without the willing sacrifice the Lord made upon the cross, that gulf would exist forever and there would be no hope for us. We would never be able to experience the love of God.

When we truly realise this, we see how different Christianity is from the ersatz cults of the New Age.

In fact, the three Abrahamic faiths, Christianity, Judaism and Islam, also recognize this difference. All three understand that sin and God are incompatible and that some repentance, some reparation, must be made for the offences and the hurt we have caused to God Himself. As Christians, we know that Jesus Himself made of His own body and blood the redeeming sacrifice that atones for the sins of all mankind, throughout the ages.

God came down to our level, because we could not ascend to His. Now that boundary is breached and the way to Him is open for all who wish it.

Nowhere in the New Age is there anything like this. On the contrary, all New Age beliefs assert that we ourselves are like God, and that in some ways we even *are* God. By certain types of meditation, pseudo-magical acts or the use of mantras, and so on, New Age followers believe they are making themselves God-like. They do not accept the very concept of sin. In this belief system, shame and guilt are consigned to the ignorance of the past.

This wilful rejection of conscience – for such it is – forms one of the chief menaces of New Age cults. After a while, the conscience becomes deadened and the sinner no longer feels remorse. God has given us all a conscience and has written His laws on our hearts, so that all societies, no matter what their religious beliefs may be, share certain ideals of behaviour and understand that transgressing is wrong. This is "natural law". We see it at work in the way that even very young children protest when something is clearly unfair, and will often share their toys or treats without being asked.

If someone continually turns away from the feeling of guilt when they know instinctively they have done something wrong, the voice of conscience is silenced. Such a situation is grave. It takes a very serious intervention from God if such a person is to be brought back to awareness.

Those who work with addicts and alcoholics will often see such a pitiful soul. People who have deadened their conscience with drugs or alcohol gradually lose all sense of guilt or shame, and the way out of their predicament seems hopeless.

Here, however, is where the truly miraculous powers of the Twelve-Step programme is most clearly seen. When worked through with care and under the direction of a sponsor, a spiritual awakening is the result, and someone who has committed grave, even mortal, sins comes to realise their plight.

With that realisation comes the recognition of the need to repent, to make reparation for the harm they have done. Since the steps are based on Christianity and are thoroughly grounded in Christ's merciful love, the recovering addict can then begin to seek God's presence and above all, His forgiveness.

All of us, whatever the nature of our sins, know that they cut us off from God, and cannot be allowed to remain. But how are we to be free of them? We cannot cleanse ourselves supernaturally. We must come before God truly contrite and humble, and beg for his forgiveness. He will take us as we are, and accept the offering of our humility and the knowledge of our littleness.

The Catholic Church has the immense grace of the sacrament of penance. We do not have to wonder whether we have "really" been forgiven. We know that we have, because when we confess to a priest we are given the blessed reassurance that God has indeed forgiven us and will restore us to full communion with Him.

How often should we confess? As often as we feel the need! And if we are living a truly Christian life, God will make us aware through our conscience when we must seek absolution for the sins we commit.

We know there is a difference of degree in our sinfulness, that some sins are more serious than others, and that the worst of all will cut off our soul and keep us permanently estranged from God unless we confess. Rather than worry needlessly about whether we have committed venial, serious or mortal sins, however, we can avail ourselves of this sacrament whenever God prompts us to do so.

Thankfully, there is no limit to the number of times we can be forgiven by God when we are truly sorry! Jesus says we must forgive our brother "seventy times seven," not as an exact mathematical calculation but to signify willingness without limits to forgive those who hurt us and who ask for our forgiveness. And, since God will never be outdone in generosity, the extent of His forgiveness towards us is immeasurable. We will never come to the end of His mercy.

Of course, when we are truly sorry we strive to make reparation for the harm we have done. Priests will give us penances, and in addition there may be many ways we can make up for the pain we have caused to others and to God, which will become clear to us from moment to moment when we live in His presence.

The first requirement for receiving forgiveness is, of course, the knowledge of our own guilt. Today, we are encouraged on all sides to let go of this concept, and this is part of the tragedy of our times.

As we have seen, the various New Age beliefs which proliferate today deny the reality of sin and guilt. Everything is permitted, nothing is condemned. The hippie view that any action is fine as long as it won't hurt anyone is truly nonsensical

– for how can we know the consequences of our actions with any certainty?

Moreover, society today is being corrupted more and more by Satan's malignancy, so much so that many people really do not know when they have committed a sin, let alone feel the need to make reparation.

Satan's aim is to steal the soul and to thwart God's plan for redemption. He therefore uses any means in his power to achieve that end, and with the dazzling array of technology available to him these days he is making huge strides towards achieving his aim.

Even those behaviours which everyone once agreed were sinful – greed, lust, gluttony, sloth and many, many more – are now seen by many as perfectly normal. If we desire someone for sexual purposes, we are encouraged to go ahead and satisfy our lust.

Our bodies are no longer thought to be temples of the Holy Spirit but objects, commodities, to be bartered in the marketplace that is today's dating scene. It is the Christian who objects to these acts who is today reviled and persecuted, as Jesus warned us that we would be.

Advertising encourages us to sin in every way possible. We must "indulge ourselves" with whatever appetite we feel, whether it be greed for food, for money, or for sexual partners. We are made to feel anxious about missing out on all the so-called good things of life unless we are youthful, attractive and sexually desirable. All these requirements mean we have to spend money and time seeking physical and mental perfection if we are to be accepted by others – and all of it is a lie.

Even worse, as we have seen, we in the West are encouraged to deny our own real culpability when our behaviour falls short of our ideals. If you have harmed someone, there will always be a New Age guru or atheist counsellor who will be ready to convince you that you really did no such thing, and that you need feel no guilt at all. It is all the fault of your parents, or your teachers, or the church. You can let yourself off the hook and go on your way, sinning as much as you like.

Many counsellors and psychiatrists are responsible, conscientious people, and a large number are Christians. I would always advise someone to seek counselling from such a therapist rather than trust myself to anyone who has been seduced by the twisted thinking of today's confused and sinful attitudes.

A knowledgeable and wise priest or Religious will often be the best person to offer advice and pastoral counselling. The abuse scandal of recent years may prevent many from seeking out a priest, but the vast majority of priests are decent, honest, holy men, and I would much rather trust my spiritual health to a priest than to a layperson with no religious beliefs.

When I was working a Twelve Step programme I made my Step Five to a priest. That step consists of making a "fearless and searching moral inventory", and because so many people now find deliverance by working the steps, many priests and Religious are trained to help them do so.

I made an appointment to see a Jesuit priest, who listened to my confession with great patience, and offered sound advice about how I might make reparation to those I had harmed through my addiction.

Because he was a priest he was able to give me absolution, and I walked out of the study feeling cleansed and renewed. A huge burden rolled from my shoulders and I knew that God had not only forgiven me, He had drawn me close to Him in a way that had not been possible for many years because of my sinfulness.

Nothing that the world can give can compare with this. It is, I believe, the "peace which passeth understanding", the reconciliation of the individual soul with its Maker, that brings indescribable joy to the pardoned sinner.

*　　*　　*

Those of us who do feel remorse for our harmful behaviours, which is – hopefully – most of us, will be completely forgiven, as long as we repent and are willing to change our behaviour. While guilt over the hurt we have done to others can be torture when we realise what we have done, we are not to wallow in it. We need to fully acknowledge what we have done and then – forgiven and restored to friendship with God – walk into the future with fresh resolve.

If we are perfectionists, if we habitually judge ourselves and others harshly and critically, we may find God's forgiveness and compassion even harder to bear than guilt. We may be tempted into believing that we somehow have higher standards than God Himself, that while He forgives us, we are not going to forgive ourselves.

Here lurks the sin of spiritual pride. When we confess and seek absolution, we are acknowledging that God is the ruler of our lives, not ourselves. If we then take back our pride and continue to judge ourselves, we are saying that we know better than Him, and we cannot agree with His mercy towards us.

A wise spiritual director, who could be a Twelve-Step sponsor, a priest, a counsellor or simply a more experienced Christian living the way we wish to live, will soon put us right. We are ordinary sinners, not specially equipped, finely-tuned sin-detectors! Acknowledging this fact means accepting our own littleness, our very creaturely nature, and it can be extremely hard for many.

Our purification is necessary before we can hope to reach Heaven. For many of us, that will be completed only after death, when we enter Purgatory. Then we will see our imperfections,

109

our blemishes, those unacknowledged sins and characteristics that keep us far from God and unfit to stand in His presence. The sufferers in Purgatory accept their pains with willingness, however, since they know that one day they will be with God, in Heaven. Remorse is a spiritual fire.

*   *   *

St. Therese is an excellent guide in this predicament.

She knows she has committed many sins, she tells us in her autobiography, but she stands before God as a "little one", and confidently expects His merciful love and His forgiveness no matter how wrongly she has behaved, as long as she stays "little".

By this, St. Therese means that we must turn to Him with the confidence of a child towards loving parents. Admitting we are wrong, and not trying to justify or defend ourselves, puts us before God in all our littleness, our helplessness without Him, and this attitude is sure to win God's compassion.

Because she emphasises the need for staying small, St. Therese's path has been called "The Little Way," or "The Way of Spiritual Childhood". When we adopt this attitude, she tells us, God will lift us up and carry us over obstacles as though we were small children unable to climb a stair by ourselves. She points out that we cannot become holy by ourselves, and must admit our need of God before He can help us.

And when we are racked with guilt, needing forgiveness but afraid to confess what we have done, her attitude of child-like confidence and acceptance is exactly what we most need to adopt.

Any loving parent knows there is nothing that our children can do which we cannot forgive. All they need do is ask, and they will be forgiven. We want them to see what they have done

110

wrong, and to be truly sorry, and when they come to us with regret for some small sin, we cannot withhold our forgiveness – we will embrace them and reassure them that all is well and they have not lost our love, that if anything, we love them all the more because of their contrition.

God is the most loving and compassionate parent of all, so when we realise that we are His children and we need to ask His forgiveness, we may be sure He will never refuse us.

St. Therese not only offered up her very real sufferings during her short life, she offered the whole of herself, her weakness, her stumbling progress, even her very life itself to the God she knew was truly her Father in Heaven.

If she had acquired any merit, she said, she did not want to keep it for herself. No, she would come before Him at the end of her life with empty hands, having given everything to Him, to use as He willed.

Her Way of Spiritual Childhood was for "little ones" like herself, like you and me. She could not possibly emulate great saints who endured terrible torments, such as being burnt alive or sent to distant lands to face martyrdom. Instead, Therese would offer daily sacrifices, whatever presented itself in her everyday, ordinary life.

The more she looked for little occasions to please Jesus, the more easily she found them. If her food was too cold or insufficient, she would not complain. She sought out the chipped jug, the poorly trimmed lamp, anything she could find in the convent's store that was imperfect and that others would not want. These she used gladly, offering her poverty to the Lord.

When a wheelchair-bound sister proved extremely difficult, constantly complaining about Therese's clumsiness in pushing her chair or grumbling about her daily hardships, Therese would greet her with a smile and kind words. Another sister always managed to splash Therese with dirty water when they were both consigned to work in the convent laundry. Not by a shudder or frown did Therese betray her natural disgust, but used this too as an opportunity to practise self-restraint and discipline.

In these little, daily sacrifices, Therese shows us how we too may use the very ordinary, everyday events and people in our lives to refine us and cleanse us of negative emotions. If we persist in this daily effort, we will find that little by little these contrarieties fail to upset us. We will become calmer, less subject to impatience, ill humour or intolerance. These are small things, but nevertheless they are what God sends us in each moment, and what He wills us to take as spiritual food.

At the end of the day, when we review our behaviour, we will see how often we have failed. Then, as Therese shows us, we must simply turn to Jesus and accept His forgiveness, His love, which He pours upon us most generously even in those moments when we fail Him the most.

Here is the secret to the Little Way – the deep, abiding humility with which we accept ourselves as we are, with all our imperfections, not seeking to excuse our lapses, and not expecting to have great achievements to present to the Lord.

Like children before a loving parent, we admit what we are and what we have done, and we confidently expect loving forgiveness from the One Who is our Heavenly Father.

So important is this last point – that we may be sure of forgiveness when we are truly sorry for our imperfect behaviours – that Maurice Nicoll, the teacher and psychiatrist we met earlier, emphasized it when he spoke about self-observation.

To observe ourselves, he reminded students, is the first and most basic step when we embark on the great work of psychological transformation.

Without knowing who we are and what we have done, there is no hope of change. He explained that there are many processes which can only take place in the dark, and when a light is shone upon them, they cease. Light itself can be cleansing and healing, and the Light of Christ the most purifying light of all.

Having seen and acknowledged our state, we simply turn to God and ask him to remove our defects. This is a stage that will be familiar to all Twelve-Step followers, and it requires that we humbly ask Him to remove all our character defects.

We can't remove them ourselves, not even by the most strenuous application of our own willpower. We can't lift ourselves up by tugging at our own feet. But God can, and will, when we ask Him, and it is then that a true healing will begin.

Always, however, we must resist the temptation to judge and criticise ourselves over what we have learned. Yes, we are full of faults, even vices; yes, we have done things which we might see as unforgivable, even the best of us. But this sort of judgement leads us nowhere but to needless suffering, as Nicoll terms it. And that is the very suffering we must sacrifice for our own good, because it stops us from truly seeing ourselves as we are.

Jesus warns us about the need to avoid judgement. He does not mean that we should pay no heed to consequences, nor that we should accept any and all sinful acts – in ourselves and in others – as perfectly fine. We must all take note of foolish and sinful behaviour, and learn as much as we can in order to avoid it ourselves, as well as steering clear of people and places that encourage us to sin.

But the critical attitudes that lead us to condemn people as hopeless cases, as unworthy human beings, are themselves sinful. Nobody has the right to judge and to condemn except God Himself, and if we habitually regard others in this way, we also condemn ourselves.

We must have compassion on others and on ourselves. And this means that never can we condemn ourselves as creatures so sinful that we deserve to be punished eternally for our faults.

If we truly repent, there is no need to go over and over what we have done, or thought, or said. Such endless condemnation is a dark corridor lined with distorting mirrors, and it leads only to utter despair.

If you find yourself judging yourself, or other people, in this way, the remedy is to firmly turn away from these futile thoughts and place yourself in the warmth and light of God's love. His Light is like the sunshine on a dark day. Allow yourself to bask in it, and to delight in the love and forgiveness that your Heavenly Father constantly sends you.

This is the Way of Purgation – self-knowledge, self-acceptance, and the abandonment to love which St Therese and many other great saints taught us.

As we gradually accept the cleansing process that constitutes this section of our spiritual journey, so we come closer to God.

In time, we begin to see that everything that has befallen us, together with all our suffering, came to us from the hand of God. He wills all that happens in our lives, either by simply permitting something painful to happen to us or by directly sending us a difficult situation because He knows we will benefit from it.

We learn to see our lives through God's eyes, as it were. We become illuminated, enlightened in our understanding of His purposes for us, and we no longer fight against each difficult situation, each cross. We believe that, like a loving parent, God will discipline us so that we become fit for the Life of Eternity, for in order to be able to dwell with Him in Heaven we must be purified on Earth.

After all, Heaven cannot possibly contain anyone given to angry impulses, or impatience, or worry. Just think of the problems that would cause – if our sinful minds, as they are right now, were to be cast in eternity. That would mean we could never be free of these tendencies, and neither would anyone else in Heaven. And that would be to turn Heaven itself into a Purgatory, or even Hell.

All those who are to live with God, with all his saints and angels, and with those we love who have in turn been purified, must be fit to occupy that state without causing any friction or unhappiness, and without those negative emotions and worrying thoughts which plague most of us on Earth.

A loving parent, seeing that a child is weak or ill, will call for appropriate treatment. That may include taking bitter medicines, practising painful exercises to strengthen wasted muscles, and undergoing extra lessons to learn how to stay fit and healthy in future.

Our God, our Father in Heaven, will do no less for us, His children on Earth.

Chapter Eight

The importance of "a good death"

Catholics have always known the importance of "a good death", which puts an end to suffering and opens the door to a happy life with God in eternity. Yet, to non-Catholics, this phrase can sound paradoxical.

How can death – which modern society regards as the ultimate evil – be "good", in any sense of the word?

Why can we not just put an end to the sufferings of the sick and elderly by granting them a peaceful end through euthanasia?

And, in a further paradox, the word "euthanasia" itself translates literally as "good death", even though to Catholics it means anything but that.

As I wrote this chapter, the world was suffering a pandemic, the coronavirus known as Covid-19. It is still present with us, and probably always will be just as influenza is, but it is no longer as likely to be fatal except among the elderly and vulnerable. It spreads very quickly, is carried on droplets in the air from a cough or sneeze as well as on surfaces, and affects both young and old.

In the face of this unknown and frightening new disease, people were told to stay home, isolate themselves from others who suffered symptoms of Covid, and to wear masks if they have to go out of the house. Many shops and businesses were closed, a situation which is now causing great economic problems for the world.

Even churches were forbidden to open, and for a long period there was no way to attend Mass.

Doctors and health officials proposed the hitherto-unthinkable: they asked elderly people who contract the illness to stay at home and accept that they cannot be treated on a ventilator – the only way to ease a patient's breathing when the disease has progressed to a severe stage.

Instead, ventilators should be kept for the younger, healthier patients who have a better chance of recovery.

Although this makes social and economic sense to a world ruled by Mammon, there was a huge outcry from older people and their families, and from many other medical personnel, who see such a triage as utterly beyond the pale of civilised practice.

Elderly people in hospitals and care homes were asked to consider placing a "Do Not Resuscitate" order on their health forms, so that strenuous efforts to revive them, in case of collapse, would no longer be made. Again, the thinking behind this reflected society's attitude towards the very old: they are useless mouths, as Hitler said, and their lives were of no value.

In fact, such "DNR" notices are quite common, certainly not limited to pandemic emergencies. Many people have them, because the sort of resuscitation attempts that might otherwise be made can involve violent crushing and electrical shocks. A large number of such patients receive broken ribs as a result, not to mention the psychological trauma that is inevitable. To the very old, this degree of injury is unacceptable, and they would rather be left in peace for what remains of their lives. But this painful decision must be left to the sick and elderly patients themselves, not to those authorities who are being urged to save money.

The emphasis placed during the pandemic on the need to sacrifice the old horrified many people, and rightly so. A Christian society has always reverenced human life in all its variety, and all lives considered equally valuable. Yet this cold-blooded calculation – of which lives to save and which to sacrifice – shows how far we have fallen from the teachings of the Bible.

Today, in normal times as well as during emergencies, we see three attitudes to death. First is the use of extreme measures to prolong life or to resuscitate the dying, even when those measures involve pain and distress to the patient.

Second is the possibility of euthanasia, already legal in a number of countries, which amounts to suicide, in order to avoid further pain and suffering.

Finally, we have what used to be universal, the acceptance of death as a part of existence, and the consequent need to prepare oneself, mentally and spiritually, for that event so that when it arrives we may face it with equanimity.

As Catholics, if our faith is sincere, we will choose the last possibility. We know that death is not the end of our existence, because after death we will face God, and where we will spend our life in eternity will depend on our state of mind at death.

That is why it is so important that Catholics should be able to receive the Last Rites from a priest. In the final moments of our lives we want to travel on to God reassured that we are in a state of grace and have nothing to fear from facing our Creator and Judge.

We need time to prepare ourselves for this event. That is why we need to ask God for the grace of a good death, that our death should not come upon us suddenly and find us unprepared because of an accident or natural disaster.

Of course, since we may be taken at any time, it's prudent to be prepared "just in case".

Such a situation may befall anyone. In my own case, I literally died in a car accident when I was 36 years old. I went through a Near Death Experience, the correct term for a journey out of our bodies while we are – temporarily – physically dead.

Those who have survived such a journey tell of very similar events. There is a dark tunnel through which we journey, and a great light which appears as we make our way through the darkness and draws us onwards. At the end of the tunnel we meet with a supernatural figure, who in my case I knew was Jesus, the source of the light itself. I felt an overwhelming compassion emanating from Him, a great sense of peace and acceptance which was so joyful and serene that I would willingly have journeyed further into that light.

As I was the mother of two young children, however, I was given a choice. I was shown their faces, and had to decide whether to continue into the light and love that waited on the other side of the tunnel, or whether to return to earthly life and be with my children.

I made the choice any parent would make: to return so that I could be with them as they grew to adulthood.

Many people have reported similar experiences. All over the world, from many different cultures, the Near Death Experience takes a similar path. The dying may see themselves, as I did at the start of the journey, looking down at their own bodies and being aware they are no longer in that body, no longer suffering what may seem like agony to onlookers unaware that the dying person's consciousness is floating above the body, free of any pain.

Some people report seeing angels at the end of the tunnel; others have seen spiritual figures from their own tradition, perhaps Moses or the Buddha. Many non-Christians have encountered Jesus for the first time, and have been shown in a flash that He is the One who has been with them all their lives, even though they did not know it.

But a good experience is not guaranteed.

Others have gone through the tunnel to face terrifying

demons. They have reported being dragged against their will towards a place of darkness and fire, crowded with repulsive figures who jeer and mock them. Like the happy experiences, these too occur to people from many different faiths or no faith at all.

Those who underwent these horrifying deaths and who have lived to speak of it have almost all amended their lives. They have returned to the practice of their faith, have adopted an ethical, moral way of life, have sought forgiveness from those they have hurt, and have abandoned their old, immoral habits.

If they recognized that the One they encountered was Jesus, as so many did, they have become Christians. If they were already nominally Christian, they have deepened their faith and their prayer life and changed their behaviour.

Those who, like me, had a positive experience have often returned to life with a very different perspective from before. I knew that my faith was real, that what awaited me after death was eternal life, and that I had the power to choose what sort of eternity I would experience.

Although Jesus was compassionate and forgiving, I saw on my return to earthly life that so much of my existence violated His commandments. I had been given a reprieve, but if I continued on what had been a sinful path I would have grieved Him beyond measure, and I could not bear to be the cause of His suffering. Now that I had truly experienced His unbounded love, I knew in the fibre of my being that I had to live in the way He wished.

As a result, I changed my way of life, one day at a time. I won't go into details here, although I have written about it elsewhere. Those who have studied the lives of people like me, those who have been given Near Death Experiences, have concluded that it can take seven years for their effects to work themselves through and manifest in a new way of life.

Some people change their ways immediately, and I attempted to do this as best I could, but it was only when, at the end of those seven years, I was received into the Catholic Church and given the power to stop drinking, that my life completely changed.

Since then, I have never doubted the existence of God and of the afterlife..

I know, from my own experience, that death is not the end of our existence. I know, too, that what our afterlife will be depends on our way of life and especially on our spiritual state at the moment we die.

All this is common knowledge in the Church, but so many – even Christians – act as though it were not true, or – if partly true – nothing to worry us here and now. We go about our everyday lives as though we will live forever, as though none of our sinful acts bear consequences, and even, thanks to delusional teaching, that God will forgive us everything in spite of our refusal to repent.

That final moment, that final repentance, is what will ultimately determine our destiny. It has been said many times that God does not send anyone to Hell – we choose Hell ourselves, because we reject God.

Yet, if we are serious about our faith, and if we meditate on the boundless compassion of Jesus, we will want to live as He asks us to do. We do not want to spend longer than necessary in Purgatory, which is a place of suffering because we see how we have fallen short of God's ideals, how we have grieved Him and harmed others in our lifetime.

Who would wish to prolong this painful state any longer than it takes for us to be purified?

What if we could, by changing our lives, change our final destiny so that our time in Purgatory will be short, kept to the bare minimum? And maybe, even, that we could attain such a state of grace at our death that we might be taken straight to Heaven? Yes, that is for the saints, but remember that we are all called to be saints. If we are called, it must be possible to achieve it. That should be our aim for the rest of our lives.

There is no suffering in life which is as great as that we shall experience in Purgatory, if we are to spend time there. The hardest part about that time will be the separation from God. We will have been in His presence and felt His love and tenderness, so we will know quite well what we are missing in Purgatory.

What is more, we shall see that it is we ourselves who have caused so much harm and hurt; we who have brought hardship and sufferings upon ourselves and those we love; we who have wounded the heart of our all-loving and all-compassionate Creator.

These sufferings compose not only the purification we need to be worthy to stand in Heaven before God, but also the temporal punishment that many of us will have to serve on account of the sins we committed during our lifetime. In Purgatory we will understand why we are there, and we will feel true remorse.

In Chapter Three, we looked at how we suffer unnecessarily in our inner life. We saw that so much of our unhappiness – that which might be called "neurotic" and which goes on unnoticed so often, like a grumbling soundtrack at the back of our minds – is completely useless. It brings us no pleasure, but can cause great harm.

It is the manifestation of inner pride, or fear, or anger towards ourselves and others that so often we neglect because it happens so frequently.

Yet it is immensely harmful.

If we persist in unconscious resentment, anxiety or a feeling of being unjustly treated, we develop ingrained attitudes that are very hard to shift.

Those in a Twelve Step programme will understand exactly what I mean. In working the Steps, we are advised to take a "spot inventory" during the day, when we notice our thoughts and feelings, and whether they are useful or harmful. At the end of each day we are recommended to cast a look back at our mental processes, and to see what the overall inner state of that day has been. We look for occasions when we have been insecure, resentful, or arrogant, and we turn these states over to the care of the God of our understanding, asking Him to remove our character defects.

Clearly, this is a well-founded Christian approach which all of us, whether in a Twelve Step programme or simply trying our best to live our often difficult lives, would do well to adopt.

In fact, the regular examination of thoughts, actions and feelings throughout the day, as well as the personal assessment at the end of the day, are practices which many spiritual leaders have taught. They are practised in Christian monasteries, by lay Christians as well as clergy, and by many Jews and Moslems as well as Buddhists. Catholics who regularly go to confession will often use this method of self-examination.

The object is not to make us depressed or unhappy, but to see where we are thinking and acting selfishly so that we have the chance to change.

Unless we know what we are like, we can never change. Sometimes, when such inward attitudes become seriously harmful, we may need to look at them with a skilled therapist or spiritual director, someone who is completely on our side and who will not condemn us, but who can see, more clearly than we ourselves can, exactly how we are hurting ourselves.

In Purgatory, the ultimate personal inventory, the most complete examination of conscience, will be necessary so that we may enter Heaven.

Imagine how dreadful our afterlife would be, if we all brought our neuroses, our resentments, our insecurities and our criticisms with us. God cannot possibly allow any of these problems to become immortal. Heaven would turn into Hell itself!

You might meet that neighbour whose noisy parties annoyed you so much, and who still irritates you. Whenever you met, you would begin to argue. And that cousin who borrowed money and never repaid it. Your resentment would fester and soon a quarrel would break out.

Worse, you could run into that haughty teacher who never gave you a grade higher than C. You forgave her as an adult, but in Heaven you find she is just as scornful of you as ever, and rebuffs every attempt to let bygones be bygones. You find yourself in a bad mood whenever you catch sight of her, and lose your temper with your family.

And so it would go on – and on – and on, just as it does in our lives on Earth, until one person realises and breaks the chain. And even then, we are powerless over other people, so they would not necessarily accept any reconciliation.

It's easy to see that, given our human nature and our fallibility, we could, if allowed in to Heaven in our imperfect state, create a nightmare for ourselves and others. There would, in fact, be no Heaven at all.

Thank God, He has designed a school for us all. That school is Purgatory.

There we can see our problems and let go of all the negativity that shapes so many lives on Earth. If we did not have this school, there would be no possibility of lasting happiness with God in Heaven. We would not dare to approach Him, aware of our sins, and would be cut off from Him for ever.

In Purgatory we will be shown just what needs to change before we are fit company for one another in eternity, and able to stand in the Presence of the Holy One. And, seeing these things in God's purifying, cleansing light, we will gladly let go of them all and consign them to forgetfulness.

They are what I have called our "False Crosses", the suffering that we were never meant to endure but which we, our parents and others have created from our own inner attitudes. They are passed on, sometimes through many generations, and their effect is very unpleasant, but the good news is that God will help us at every occasion as we freely let go and allow His light to heal us.

We will at last be free of all their effects, inwardly reborn, and made ready to live with Jesus, Mary and all the saints in the everlasting joy of eternity.

However hard it will be to see ourselves in this light, we will know, even in the midst of our pain and separation, that one day we will surely be in Heaven. We will know that eventually, after we have undergone this purification, we will be with God in a state of eternal blessedness. This state is called the Beatific Vision, and the knowledge that it awaits us will comfort and sustain us during our time of suffering in Purgatory.

For this reason, we refer to those in Purgatory as Holy Souls. They are on their way to Heaven, having won the battle on Earth. They need no longer fear the greatest suffering of all, that of Hell, where there is no possibility of ever getting out.

The Church recommends us to pray for the Holy Souls. We are told that they know when we pray for them, and if we ask a priest to offer a Mass on their behalf there is great rejoicing and a shortening of their sufferings there.

Here on Earth, when we pray and when we offer up our own suffering, God may use it to help another soul on the other side of the world who is suffering and in a worse state than ourselves;

as Christians we are part of a universal community dedicated to loving God and loving His people, who help one another as we ourselves long to be helped during our own suffering. This is what the Church calls "the communion of saints", and we are all potential members of that loving society.

The Holy Souls are just as much a part of that community – the Communion of Saints – as those here on Earth and the Saints in Heaven. As we pray for them, so they can pray for us and help us. When we eventually reach Heaven, we may be greeted by any number of people who will tell us how our own prayers and sufferings have helped them to attain blessedness.

I believe it will be a little like the film, "It's a Wonderful Life," in which a suicidal young man is shown how, eventually, his own life will have helped many others, and how greatly loved he is, even by people he never knew personally on Earth.

If this is so, and if we are truly part of the Communion of Saints, how marvellous that experience will one day be, when in Heaven we meet those we have helped, and those who have helped us, without our ever knowing it during our lifetime here.

*   *   *

For many of us our Purgatory begins on Earth.

In Chapters Three and Four we looked at the inescapable suffering that is everyone's lot in life. We saw that when we accept everything as coming from God, for our ultimate benefit and so that we have something of great value to offer Him when we carry our real cross, then our suffering is transformed.

Whether it be physical or emotional pain, if we offer it in reparation for our sins and for the sins of others, we give Jesus and Mary a spiritual treasure which they will use for our benefit and for the benefit of people we may never know until we meet them one day in Heaven.

126

It is not always possible to make this offering with clarity of mind, but if it has become our habit during better times to offer our whole selves every day to God, that

practice will become so ingrained that when suffering becomes too intense for thought - as it may one day happen – our silence and our acceptance of that cross will speak to God in the language of the heart.

For Catholics, that knowledge is part of our education, and examples are shown us by great saints, such as St. Therese of Lisieux and Mother Angelica, the foundress of EWTN who lived the final part of her life with great physical suffering but offering all to God.

For others, however, who may have only the weakest faith or no faith at all, the thought of physical suffering and death is abhorrent.

They see no value in suffering, and this attitude is reinforced at every turn by our materialistic society.

If there is no God, if there is no Heaven, then why should we accept the need to suffer in order to transform ourselves and help others? If there is nothing at the end of life but unconsciousness, then why not eat, drink and be merry, and the consequences be damned?

To those who have never considered the spiritual side of suffering – and this includes the followers of shallow New Age philosophies which promise rewards and prosperity if they adopt the "right" thoughts and feelings – suffering and death mean only failure.

If they suffer disease, it is their own fault; they have not correctly carried out the various New Age formulae for health, wealth and success.

Of course, this is not the Christian approach – nor the attitude of any genuine spiritual path – but it is peddled relentlessly even by those who should know better, the tele-evangelists along with the white magic brigade, and thoughtlessly adopted by millions today.

When they are in pain and facing death, the logical procedure, according to this attitude, is to ask for an assisted suicide. And in this, they are backed by all materialists, including some in the medical profession, who see such lives as having no value.

If you are old, if you are suffering an incurable disease which you know will grow more painful over time, then why not put an end to your life in a relatively painless manner and spare yourself more suffering?

Increasingly in our time these possibilities are being pushed relentlessly at the old, the chronically sick and the disabled.

In some European countries this way of death has become so widely accepted that it is not even debated any more. You may travel to Switzerland and drink a cup of legally sanctioned poison in the presence of your loved ones, and make a painless exit.

In Belgium and the Netherlands, many doctors routinely consider this option for their patients whom medicine can no longer cure. It is a frightening new reality, and even more terrible when it is applied to men and women whose minds have been wounded through dementia or severe depression.

Some have said they felt pressured to ask for euthanasia so they would not be a burden to society. Others have told of their wish not to be dependent on family members, or simply to avoid more pain.

A Dutch "end of life" clinic has registered a sharp increase in the number of patients asking to be put to death by its medical staff. In 2019, 898 patients – about 30 percent of those who applied – were killed by its team of euthanasia experts. The clinic says this number showed a 22 percent increase over previous years, which they say is due to the fact that euthanasia is now becoming widely accepted in Europe.

Many demands are made by patients with dementia, or – more worryingly – by their families or carers. A particularly shocking example of the "death clinic" procedures was that of an elderly woman with Alzheimer's disease. Her death was filmed by television cameras, and the procedure was deemed to be completely lawful.

A second, similar, woman's death was reported by the clinic, which had carried out the legal killing while the patient was vigorously resisting the injection, but who was said to be incapable of expressing her wishes because of her dementia. Th ese cases have been widely reported, and you can read more about them on Christian websites.

Compare this materialistic attitude to human life, and the willingness to inflict death on someone considered "useless" by society, to that shown by Mother Teresa of Calcutta.

In her Kalighat Home for the Dying Destitutes, which has been renamed the "Kalighat Home of the Pure Heart", Mother Teresa's nuns give their patients the opportunity to die with dignity, according to the rites of their faith. Muslims are read passages from the Koran; Hindus are given water from the Ganges; and Catholics receive the Last Rites.

"A beautiful death," said Mother Teresa, "is for people who lived like animals to die like angels – loved and wanted."

When we read these different accounts, we know instinctively, we understand with our inmost heart, that dying is not about extinguishing life by external means. No man or woman, however sick or destitute, deserves to be put to death as a matter of convenience.

Hitler's death squads inflicted their terrible ends on sick and disabled people, whom they called "useless mouths". They killed those they thought were of inferior races, and treated them like so much garbage to be disposed of and buried or burnt. Euthanasia is not so very different from Hitler's squads. It is dressed up and prettified, but it is essentially on the same continuum.

In the face of such horrors we have to assert once more that human beings are not animals, and our death is the most significant event in our lives.

All doctors know about palliative care. Modern medicines can relieve even the worst pain, and nobody needs to suffer in this way.

Death can be peaceful. It can and should be pain-free, because facing the passage from this world to the next is a tremendous experience, one for which the patient needs to be completely prepared and in as comfortable a state as possible. At this point, our total offering to God, including the complete acceptance of suffering throughout our life and our faithful efforts to follow Christ's teaching, is made once and forever.

Knowing this, our death can be accepted with equanimity and become what it should always be – a spiritual transition that fulfils one's destiny.

Whether someone dies in a hospice setting, in a care home, or in his or her own home, drugs can keep pain from becoming overwhelming and allow the sick person to depart this life peacefully and in harmony with their own beliefs.

Anyone, no matter what their illness or state of mind, can today have a plan for their own death which includes relief from pain and the complete absence of any pressure to hasten the process.

Knowing that one's end is in sight can be a huge blessing. The patient has time to make peace with their families and other loved ones, and peace with their God. A priest may be alerted to the possibility of imminent death so that a last confession can be made, and the eucharist offered. Such a death is a fitting end to life, not a degradation or an unimaginable horror.

It is far better than being taken suddenly in a state of unreadiness, without having made a confession and with no chance of the Last Rites. Catholics pray for the grace of "final penitence", and that they may be spared an unprepared death. The Last Rites, the viaticum, are supremely important, and in an emergency they can be administered by any Catholic priest, wherever they may be.

What, then, is "final penitence"? And why is it so important?

The reason Catholics pray for this is because, even if we cannot make a last confession, our inner state at the moment of death will decide our destiny, whether we go to Heaven or Hell.

If we die impenitent, if we have not felt true contrition for our sins during our lifetime and if, even at the moment when we are to meet God we refuse to accept any responsibility for what we have done and to feel remorse, then we are surely bound for Hell. God will not have put us there, it is we who will have chosen it by our attitude.

The moment we die is the most important moment of our entire lives, because it decides where we will spend eternity.

We will be given the chance to choose God or to reject Him, and that choice will be final.

We cannot judge whether any individual has been sent to Hell. We simply do not know. We are not God, and we can have no idea in what state somebody has lived their final moment on Earth.

I say "usually", because there are sometimes hopeful signs. St. Therese was given the grace of knowing that Pranzini, a notorious murderer for whose soul she prayed, had kissed a crucifix three times before he was executed. She knew this meant he would eventually reach Heaven, and thanked God for this knowledge.

In Evelyn Waugh's "Brideshead Revisited", a character makes a similar gesture, and although he has lived a very sinful life, the family are reassured that he will some day be in Heaven.

But what of others, whose final moments we can never know? What of murderers, dictators, adulterers, thieves? Even if they have committed terrible crimes, and even though we cannot imagine that such a person will be saved, it is still true that a final act of remorse, of contrition, a knowledge that the sinner has offended God and is truly sorry, will be enough to save them from Hell.

The problem is that we cannot know whether such a penitence was ever granted. Therefore, we cannot judge others, but we must always prepare ourselves for this possibility, and live our lives in such a way that God in the end will receive us for the sake of His Son, who loves each and every person as dearly as though they were the only person in the world. He does not will the damnation of anyone, but He cannot prevent some from choosing it, incomprehensible though such a choice is.

We shall now look at some of the ways we can make the inevitable end to our life "a good death".

*   *   *

First, we need to prepare for our death every day of our lives. I don't mean that we should become morbid or fearful; quite the opposite. We can practice daily prayer and meditation so that our friendship with God is strong. Doing so regularly, not just as an occasional event, shapes our minds and ensures that we will be ready to meet Him on that fateful day.

Here on Earth we know how important it is to prepare ourselves beforehand for a meeting with someone in authority – a boss, a supervisor, a lawyer, and so on. You would not want to meet that person without understanding all the facts of your situation and making sure you have carried out the tasks you were given to the best of your ability.

If you have neglected your prayer life, you will one day find yourself unprepared for the all-important meeting with the One who created you and showed you how to live. Your death, and the subsequent assessment of your life by your Creator, will be much more difficult if you have not learned who He is, and what He requires from you.

We need to ask ourselves what a good prayer life would look like. How can we pray and meditate with sincerity, so that we achieve that equanimity and inner peace which all of us yearn for, whether consciously or not?

The "peace which passeth all understanding", the wholehearted welcome and acceptance of everything in our life as coming from God, will accompany us through every stage of our physical death and our entrance in the afterlife. To reach this state of grace we must prepare ourselves each day. Then, if we should find we are called home this very moment, we will not face our Creator unprepared.

Spiritual life is sometimes compared to a staircase. We take one step at a time, to use the language of Twelve Step groups, and don't try to run up the whole flight in one breathless dash.

Fortunately, God Himself has given us some very clear instructions on prayer as well as on daily living, and the church has many great traditions in her treasury. Following them, we will find our days yield much harvest.

Here, I'd like to offer some tentative suggestions. Your life will not be exactly like mine, of course, nor will it be identical with anyone else's circumstances. But there are some guidelines we can all use, adapting to our individual situation as necessary.

Morning prayer is the foundation for the rest of our day.

We may begin each day by reciting the Lord's Prayer. It is a prayer that you may say together with others or alone, as your circumstances allow, but the important thing is to pray! And the Lord's Prayer is the very finest model of prayer that we can possibly have, since it was given to us by God Himself.

Personally, I'm not a morning person, and have to keep things very simple as I wake from sleep. The next step, for me and for many others, is to pray to Our Lady with the Hail Mary prayer. It is a such a short prayer that anyone can say it, but so profound that it centres us and prepares us for the fact that we will one day pass away, and will need the prayers of Our Lady as we face that moment.

Of course, you will want to add your personal prayers for your own needs, the needs of your family, for your neighbours, and for the world.

Again speaking personally, I find daily meditation is a necessity. Without it, I simply don't have the strength to meet the demands of each day. I know from experience that I will burn out faster unless I have set time aside each morning to meet with God one-to-one, to listen to His wisdom and receive the grace He sends me to cope with my circumstances, whatever they may be.

To prepare myself for this time, I like to read a passage or two from Scripture first, musing on each word or phrase, and opening myself to their meaning. This practice, known as "lectio divina", is a centuries-old tradition among Religious congregations, and a number of books have been published on how to read the Bible in this way, so I will not enlarge on it here.

Then comes my time of silence before the Lord, the most solemn and important moments of my day.

Your situation will undoubtedly differ from mine. As you begin your spiritual journey towards the meeting with God, ask Him what prayers and practices He wants you to assume. He will guide you without fail, and the more you listen to Him the closer you will become to His Heart, and the more peace and joy you will find accompanying you on your way.

If you are not sure how to begin this journey, you might wish to consult your parish priest or someone else whose spiritual life you admire, perhaps a friend or a member of a religious order. There are many books available today which outline what a simple Rule of Life looks like. Don't take on too much, however. Begin with prayers and practices you feel comfortable with, and allow the Lord to lead you gently closer to Him, one step at a time.

It is a great blessing to find a good spiritual director, and if this is your need, then pray for it to be met. There have been times in my life when I have been fortunate to have wonderful spiritual direction, and others in which I've been left on my own. For beginners in prayer, direction is a tremendous help, but don't think that you absolutely have to have this in order to grow in spirit. God has left us His instruction book and the many wise counsels of the Church and His saints, and they often suffice.

As well as a strong prayer foundation, we also need the sacraments. If you are able, receive the Eucharist daily; if you cannot do this, then weekly; if illness or disability prevents you from attending Mass at all, then make a spiritual communion at home or wherever you happen to be.

Some priests are able to make regular visits to the housebound members of their parish, and will offer Confession as well as the Eucharist. But many priests cannot do so because of the pressure of their work, as well as the fact that they often have responsibilities for more than one parish. If this is your situation, then learning how to make a spiritual communion will be a vital part of your relationship with God.

Many chronically ill or disabled Catholics are left without the grace of the sacraments, perhaps for long periods of time. As I write, churches have been closed around the world because of the pandemic, and as a result, many of us – healthy or not – have had to learn to make perfect acts of contrition before asking the Lord for a spiritual communion.

In fact, spiritual communions may be made at any time, even several times a day according to your needs. They do not replace attendance at Mass, and each time we make this request we must also have the intention of going to church as soon as we are physically able to do so.

A very important part of prayer for many Catholics is the daily Rosary. Our Lady has asked us to pray the Rosary each day, and many spiritual giants have told us how helpful and even necessary this practice is for all who want to draw closer to Mary. What's more, Mary has requested that we do this, to make reparation for the sins of mankind and for blasphemies against her.

We don't know exactly how she will use the spiritual energies we dedicate to her when we pray this ancient prayer, but we know that she does not lie, and if she tells us they are beneficial, then we may believe her and obey her wishes.

If you can find a spare twenty minute slot in your day, this is ideal. You'll then be able to pray five decades of the Rosary, and not only will this answer Mary's request, you will find your own peace of mind and tranquillity greatly increased as you do so.

If you can't spare even this amount of time – and some days are much more rushed than others – then even praying one decade will be very worthwhile. Or you might decide to follow the example of Padre Pio and others, both saints and ordinary Catholics, who pray the Rosary whilst doing other things.

You don't even have to use a Rosary chain. It is very helpful because it lets you keep count of your prayers and to know where you are in a particular decade, but there are rosary rings which you can wear during the course of the day, which do the same thing. If necessary, use your fingers, although personally I find it much harder to remember where I am in the decade unless I use a Rosary.

Padre Pio was often seen with a Rosary and he prayed it constantly. We can't all manage this, but we can certainly try to pray as we work through simple chores or are travelling, or sitting in a waiting room.

Finally, I recommend a practice which reaches back far into the early age of Christianity: that of pausing during the day and noticing our state of mind.

The way I learned to do this, and which I still follow today, is to set times for pausing my activities and then observing myself just as I am – not trying to alter what is going through my mind, but just seeing it and mentally noting them. I like to choose times that are easy to remember, such as 9 a.m., 12 noon, and 5 p.m.

It just takes a few minutes to note what thoughts and feelings are passing through my mind, and then turning aside from them to remember that I am in the presence of God. For a brief time, just as long as necessary to refocus my attention away from the world and my own mundane thoughts and place them with the Lord, I belong to Him totally, body and mind and heart.

Then, when I am truly centred in Him, I go back to whatever I was doing, with the awareness that He is there, within me as well as without, and I am lifted into a better place.

Years of practice have shown me how necessary this practice of recollection is to my continued peace of mind. Days when I have to rush through these times, or when I have forgotten to do it at all, are days that can be full of anxiety and fretfulness over little problems, and yet it takes so little time to remember where

I am and in Whose Presence I stand.

I mentally "set" these pauses during my morning prayers, but if I know I am going to have the sort of day that means I won't be able to keep to them, I change them accordingly. For example, if I have to be in a meeting, or am going to lunch with a friend, I change my times of recollection to fit in with that. The important thing is to make daily "appointments with myself", which then become appointments with God.

You will learn a great deal about yourself if you decide to take up this practice. As well as calming you, and filling you with the peace which the Lord will give you even in the midst of great turmoil, you will see how you habitually react to daily events and people.

These insights will help you as you get to grips with the suffering in your life, especially the type I've called "unnecessary suffering". I have found myself sometimes worrying about events that happened years ago, things I had said and done to other people and that they had said and done to me – up to a decade earlier! All that was completely unnecessary, of course, and led me to consciously offer up these events and the people in them to the loving care of Our Father in Heaven.

I have noticed, too, how I worry unnecessarily about future problems which never actually come to pass, and how angry or anxious I can become due to these imaginary situations.

These insights are tremendously valuable, because I then start to notice how little trains of thought, throughout the day, can lead to greater fears and worries, and when I realise what is going on, I am able to stop them before they grow into big problems.

I could not do this by myself, but as long as I keep my morning prayer and meditation times I find that God gives me exactly the graces I need to become more conscious and more aware during the everyday tasks of life.

A wise spiritual director whom I had the privilege of knowing for many years advised me to read "The Practice of the Presence of God", by Brother Lawrence, a Carmelite Brother. When I did so, I saw how my daily disciplines could help me grow closer to the blessed state where I could realize that Presence more and more.

The spiritual path we can all follow does not eliminate all suffering, for that is not the goal. Some suffering is necessary and will result in a greater good as long as we accept it from the hand of God. But so much is completely useless! How much energy and time we waste in useless negative thoughts and negative emotions! How much more free we will feel if we can be free of them, and how much more useful to God and those around us!

This daily journey towards God through the acceptance of suffering is what mystics have called the Way of Purgation. They assure us that if we willingly walk this path, we will gradually experience more and more illumination in our daily lives and draw ever closer to our Creator and Lord. Eventually, we may be privileged to live in the Way of Illumination, and I believe this stage may be reached by anyone who is willing to observe themselves, as outlined above, and turn their thoughts and emotions over to the loving care of their Father in Heaven.

The final stage in this lifelong progress, for those who persevere, will be living in a state of Unity with God. Great saints have all reached this state. So have countless numbers of men and women, known and unknown, throughout the ages. It is entirely possible that we will one day be among them.

If we can live in the Presence of God, death can have no fears for us. The particular form of suffering which is how many people view their own demise becomes instead a gateway through which we must pass in order to stand in the Light of Christ, fully and face to face, in the next life.

In the wonderful book "A Time to Die," by Nicolas Diat, monks explain their attitudes towards death, and the author describes the various ways different monks died. All had peaceful, calm passings, and being present at the death of a religious brother was a tremendously inspiring spiritual experience for all their fellows in the monastery.

One of the abbots interviewed by Diat says that he has accompanied some twenty monks during their deaths.

"He has never witnessed any spectacular death agonies," Diat says. "The monks were serene and peaceful. One might speak of progressive stages. They let go, little by little, in increments, supported by the prayer of their brothers ... the threshold for tolerance changes. The monk accepts things that seemed impossible a few weeks before".

*   *   *

St. Therese faced death with equanimity, yet she feared "not being able to die" when the time came. When in great pain, as was often the case in her last weeks, she sometimes expressed the wish for her life to end.

When a doctor praised her patience, Therese exclaimed, "How can he say I am patient!" She added, "O my God, my God, I cannot go on, have mercy, have mercy on me!"

I find it very reassuring that such a great saint would give way to her pain at times, and ask God to take her. It shows that she was human, not an angel but a real person suffering in her body and in her mind. Despite these moments, she would eventually return to a calmer state, and when she realised her lapses, she would express her sorrow for how she had behaved.

At the same time, she was reassured that she was still "little".

She would not become vain about her endurance; God had made sure of that.

"How happy I am," she said, shortly after the exclamation quote above, "to find myself, even so close to death, so imperfect and so needing God's grace!"

Therese's death came after a long period of dependence and severe illness. She did not die as quickly as she had hoped, and endured spells of choking and gasping for breath towards the end. She thought she would not be able to die, that God wanted her to suffer more, and although sorely tested, she said, "I do not wish to suffer less!"

In reading these accounts, we need to remind ourselves that Therese lived almost 150 years ago. Medical science was far less advanced, and most of the painkillers we use today were unknown in her time. Although one doctor thoughtfully prescribed morphine to relieve her distress, the Mother Superior forbade Therese to take it. To us, this seems like sheer cruelty, but it was done with the best intentions: if God willed suffering, then the religious must suffer to their utmost.

While some mortification of the flesh is helpful to our spiritual progress, such as the fasting and abstinence we practise in Lent and Advent, we should never be left in such severe pain as St Therese was. It is one thing to give up chocolate, or smoking, and contribute our savings to charity. It is quite another to force someone to endure extreme pain when pain-killers are readily available, and are part of God's loving provision for us on Earth.

Today, we realise such denial is harmful. None of the abbots in Diat's book refused to let the monks use painkillers. They did try to make sure that no monk was heavily sedated for long periods, because this did nothing to help the monk prepare for death and merely prolonged their illness.

As St Therese's final moments approached, she looked at her

crucifix and said, "Oh, I love Him! My God, I love You!"

The nuns noticed that in her last minutes on Earth, her face relaxed and bore an expression of great bliss "for about the space of a Credo".

Then she was gone, her soul released from her suffering body, and we may be sure she was gathered into the arms of her waiting parents, and beyond them, to God Himself.

*   *   *

The deaths of great saints are sometimes peaceful, like those of the monks in Diat's book, and sometimes difficult. Martyrs of the Church have died in the midst of torture, through beheadings, through being starved, and in other ways that involve great physical suffering. St Peter was crucified upside down, because he did not feel worthy of emulating Jesus's example.

Such violent deaths are, today, the exception rather than rule – and for this, we may all be thankful. Yet, even in our time, Christians in other countries are being tortured and killed for their faith. The sufferings of the persecuted church continue, and may well get worse before Christ returns.

One factor unites all these deaths, however: acceptance.

As the Big Book of Alcoholics Anonymous says, acceptance is the answer to all our problems. No matter how seemingly impossible our task may be, no matter how much we may fear death, we know that anxiety and resistance will make things worse.

Many, perhaps most, of us will die peacefully in our beds, whether in hospital or at home, but it is absolutely certain that we will, some day, have to face our own mortality.

The more we accept this seemingly unpalatable fact, the simpler our lives will be. It is not to be feared, because we know that Christ will accompany us every step of the way, just as He has done during our life's whole journey from beginning to end.

Scripture assures us that there is nowhere we can go and nothing that can happen that is able to separate us from the love of God; only if we wilfully refuse that love are we left alone, and that is by our own choice. No Christian will be abandoned by Jesus, even – and especially – when we come to the moment of yielding our soul into His care.

The regular practice of the Presence of God will accustom us to this knowledge, so that in our last extremity our death may be a simple placing of our body and soul into the care of the One who has guided us and accompanied us without fail.

All of our life has in fact been a preparation for this supreme moment.

Meeting it serenely and with a good conscience, we know we are destined for eternal happiness with God and His saints. We have nothing to fear from death, and everything to gain from ensuring we undergo this final trial clean in heart and mind, and centred on the Lord.

Chapter Nine

Practising what we have learned

When we are in the midst of intense suffering, we can't suddenly adopt a new attitude to what we're going through. Pain shouts with a voice so loud that it drowns out the whispers of our soul. The best way to learn to handle suffering is to live in a different way during the times we are free from it, or at least when it abates, so that we can think clearly and make good decisions.

For this reason, beginning a new way of life, growing closer to God, is a task to undertake during the times when pain is less insistent.

By "pain", I include, throughout this book, both physical and mental pain. Obviously, someone in severe physical pain and possibly on strong pain-killers is in no position to take up a new prayer life. It is impossible. If we are in that situation, all we can do is to remember God's presence, however remote He may seem, and remind ourselves that He is there, sharing our suffering. Simply breathing in and out, holding on to the thought of God, is all we can do at these times, as I know from experience.

When I was in the utmost pain and drifting in and out of consciousness, lying in my hospital bed with no idea of when or how my suffering would end, I found the most relief when I pictured myself being held in the palm of the Father's hand.

Our Father in Heaven has immense, immeasurable love and compassion. He does not judge us in our extremity. He holds us in the hollow of His great hand, and bears our pain with us. To know this and to actually experience myself as being held safely by Him was what got me through the worst times.

Such a response will be easier if, at times of less suffering, we have begun to think of God more and more, and to practise His presence in our daily life. I cannot overstress the need to draw up – and adhere to as far as circumstances and our situation allow us – a simple Rule of Life.

When we follow such a Rule, we begin to live so that every moment of our day is sanctified and hallowed, offered to God. It does not matter whether we are washing handkerchiefs, like St Therese, changing a baby's diaper, tidying our desk, or cooking a meal for our family. Nothing is too mundane to be offered to God. Every moment, every action, may become sacred if we so wish.

In Chapter Eight I suggested practices that can anchor us in the life of the spirit and lead to closer union with God. These include daily morning and evening prayer; reading Scripture with attention and care; immersing ourselves in the writings of saints such as St Therese, who have travelled this path before us; setting times to remember the Presence of God; and – most importantly – making frequent use of the sacraments.

If we adopt regular daily prayers and times of remembrance, getting to know ourselves thoroughly so that we can ask God for the grace to deal with mental problems before they become large enough to hurt us, and if we practise contemplation so that we can "let go and let God" in our everyday life, we will be much better equipped to face suffering with equanimity.

In a busy world it can seem very difficult, even impossible, to set aside times for simply being with God, for reading about Him and paying attention to His Presence in our lives. Once we step outside our home, everything in our environment seems to conspire to push us off-centre, away from God, into the chaos and noise of the modern world.

The busy traffic, the constant background chatter of conversations around us, the insistence of the radio or Muzak in public spaces, all tend to stifle the inner voice of our interior life, which is where we meet God.

Especially today, the ubiquity of smartphones and the internet constantly act as distractions to tempt us away from our centre. The devil is the Prince of the Airwaves, which includes the internet and all electronic communications, and he is extremely clever and subtle in the way he uses them to turn our thoughts away from God and towards the temptations of this world.

I think this is the reason that St Paul advised us to "put on the whole armour of God" every single day. He did not have to deal with much of what today's world throws at us in the way of intrusive noise and constant physical assaults on our senses, but even in his time it was all too easy to become caught up in the mess and confusion of the outside world.

As a saint, and inspired by Christ, he could see further ahead, and could write for all time. What he tells us to do, in the imagery of a knight's armour, is to surround ourselves with the truths and knowledge of Scripture and – in our day – to be mindful of what the Church teaches, so that we have a deep well of understanding from which to draw in our times of trial.

Living through each day simply, setting aside times for prayer, reading and recollection as outlined in the previous chapter, can become our personal Rule of Life. If we are able, daily Mass attendance is highly desirable. One of the most difficult trials is to be unable to get to Mass, as is all too frequent for people like me, physically challenged and often in pain.

Spiritual communions are a great blessing for those of us in this situation, as we have noted, and they may be made every day, even during Mass itself when we are able to attend.

And although the noise and endless chatter of the radio and television – not to mention the distractions of the internet – can be confusing and irritating, we may all thank God for the Eternal Word Television Network, the Catholic station founded by Mother Angelica. Because of her wonderful work, we may watch Mass every day, and make a Spiritual communion as we do so.

Even non-Catholics can find inspiration in the many programmes of EWTN, which range from documentaries on saints and the religious life to discussion programmes with many different guests, and I can't recommend this station too highly.

*   *   *

Looking more deeply into the work we ourselves can do to prepare ourselves for whatever life may throw at us, I'd like to suggest a simple list of do's and don'ts; obviously some will appeal to you more than others, but I hope you may find at least some which speak to your situation.

First, the "do's":-

(1) An exercise which has helped many is to write your own memoirs. If you don't like the idea of writing, or are not physically able to do this, recording them orally, or using a computer programme which allows you to talk and then converts the speech into writing, would be invaluable. The point of this exercise is not to produce a piece of literature, but to allow you to reflect on the events of your own life, and what you have learned in your spiritual journey so far. Start at any point you wish, although one's own birth is always a good beginning! Write about your childhood, your earliest memories, the events of your life that have shaped you and brought you to this point. You will begin to see patterns of thought and behaviour in the way you react to circumstances, and will see which have helped you and brought you closer to God, and which have propelled you further away from Him.

147

In the same way as the daily inventory helps you locate yourself and understand better how you habitually think, feel and act, the memoir you write will reveal larger patterns. It will give you clues as to what may be lacking in your spiritual life, and what has brought you inner comfort. In showing you these, it will help you when you undergo future trials.

(2) When you are in good health, and life is less stressful, write your own obituary. Ask yourself what you would like people to know about you, and how you have handled the various problems you have encountered. What has helped you in your sufferings, and what would you like others to take from your own example? This can be a very enlightening exercise, and can help you to see yourself more objectively. Do it when you are well, and when you are feeling positive. It will help you to become more centred in the midst of daily life.

(3) Reflect on the good that your sufferings will surely bring. This book has tried to show you how everyone, through the painful events in our lives, has something of tremendous value to offer God, through the sufferings of Jesus of the Cross. When we unite ourselves to Him in His sorrowful Passion, we are in a very real way sharing His own sufferings, and helping Him to transform our lesser pains into something of great worth.

We have seen how suffering can transform us, how it can help us to become the saints we are all called to be. The world sees only pain and distress, the negative aspects of suffering, but as Catholics we know that God is in charge of our lives and that He can, and will, bring much good out of our sorrows. As before, this practice is better kept for times when you are in less pain, whether that is mental or physical. Then, when trials come again, you will have this knowledge on which to depend, and it will help you to endure them.

Most importantly of all, we have seen how suffering that is willingly accepted and borne cheerfully is taken up by God and used for His own transforming work. We will see in Heaven how our patient suffering has brought great good to others through the mysterious workings of God's supernatural economy. It is as though our personal afflictions, when taken in the right way, become valuable currency that God uses to help others.

St. Therese was able to feel grateful to God for the suffering He sent her, and although she never asked for it to increase – because she saw how that would be presumptuous – she expressed her gratitude by her acceptance, and by her confidence that God was using it for good. If we are able to come to such a realization, it will totally transform our attitudes to pain and difficulties.

If we practise daily prayer and recollection, we will grow in our love of God and those around us. We will be willing to endure harder times because we are aware that God's loving, fatherly hand is in all the events of our life, including those we would rather not have.

Keep in mind that, whatever it may be, your cross is the one that God designed especially for you, because it will give you the best opportunity to grow in knowledge and love for Him. He knows how much we can bear, and if it seems we have been given too heavy a load to carry, we can still be confident that He will give us the courage and strength that we need to do so.

(4) Keep a spiritual journal. Like the exercises of writing your memoirs and composing your own obituary, it will give you tremendous insights into your daily state. Each and every one of us has a daily spiritual pilgrimage to undertake, whether we are aware of it or not. It is very enlightening to look back on a spiritual journal that we have kept for a while, and see how far we have come. It may vary from one or two simple paragraphs to a page or so of journaling, although more than that could be tiring and counter-productive. Once you have begun this habit, you will find it invaluable in showing where you are with God, what you have learned, and what He is trying to do, for you and

with you, in your daily life.

(5) Remember you have the help of Our Lady and all the saints in heaven to help you when you feel unable to cope; the mother of Our Lord, especially, understands suffering and is always ready to listen to you and come to your aid. In times of great distress, I have always found the Rosary very comforting, along with special devotion to Our Lady of Sorrows. This practice has fallen out of favour in modern times, but it is very powerful and has brought many souls closer to the Immaculate Heart of Mary.

Through your own suffering, you have become an expert on pain. This expertise can be of great help to those who are also suffering, and who do not know of the treasure that their suffering may become. You are an expert because you have lived through pain yourself, and you can now empathise with others undergoing this trial. Your suffering may have been different from theirs, perhaps because you went through mental pain while someone else is experiencing physical pain, or the other way around; but even so, you are now better able to show them compassion because you yourself have suffered, and you know exactly how it feels. If the sufferer is a Christian, you now have the chance to tell them of the value of redemptive suffering.

Reading the life of St. Therese completely transformed my life. It brought me back to the arms of Jesus and into the Church He founded. You may be used by Him to help another in just such a situation. What a blessing that would be!

Now for three "don'ts" :-

(1) Don't compare yourself to others. To those with truly severe disabilities, others' relatively minor physical or mental problems may seem less serious. All our crosses are different, however, and all are tailored exactly to fit us by God Himself. He knows what we can bear, and where our limitations are. An arthritic ankle or a worry over a child's job may seem relatively

negligible to you, but in reality could affect the sufferer profoundly. What's more, people often don't share the extent of their problems, especially in Western cultures, including North America and the United Kingdom. Many of us, this writer included, have been trained to keep a "stiff upper lip" and not to burden others by telling them of our difficulties. It's therefore impossible to judge how another person is feeling, and we shouldn't try. Admittedly, this can be difficult. When I first met someone with just such an occasional arthritic twinge, she immediately claimed to "know how I felt", because her ankle bothered her from time to time. I have arthritis and nerve damage, cannot walk unaided, and suffer severe nerve and joint pain. My immediate response to this lady's well-meant remark was indignation – how could she possibly compare her own problems to mine! Fortunately, I kept my mouth shut; nobody knows the extent of another's pain, and although I felt my disability was misunderstood, there was no point in saying so. Always exercise discretion when comparing your own state to someone else's, and you won't go wrong.

(2) Don't give in to anxiety or fear concerning your situation, whatever it may be. Yes, your problems may truly seem enormous, but we are in God's hands, and those hands are constantly upholding and supporting us. Those of us who are parents know that, as our children grow towards maturity, they need more challenges if they are to reach their full potential. We don't leave the training wheels on their bicycles once they are ready to go without them; we insist they finish their homework, even when it is difficult and their friends are outside, playing. Just so does God parent us. In the words of Padre Pio, a man with exceptionally daunting sufferings, we should learn to "Pray, hope and don't worry". Practise turning every problem over to Our Lord, as He asks us to do, for he assures us that "My yoke is easy, and my burden is light". He will join us in our suffering and transform it from base lead to purest gold, but we must first ask Him to do so. We may have to repeat our offering many times during the day, but if done sincerely and trustingly, He will comfort us and aid us without fail.

(3) Don't lose heart. Some of us are more prone to mood swings than others. I am bi-polar, and could easily slip into depression if I did not keep watch over my thoughts and feelings. When I remain vigilant, I see the harmful ideas and moods before they actually begin to take over my mind, and I turn them over immediately to Our Lord. These mood swings and negative thoughts come straight from the Evil One, but they cannot do us any harm if we stop them in their tracks. Others, who may be calmer and less anxious by nature, can also feel discouraged when trials seem to go on for too long and God seems far away. You may even experience a "Dark Night", and if so, you are in excellent company. St Therese of Lisieux and Mother Teresa are two of those who underwent this severe trial at times in their journey. If you are afflicted in this way, seek counselling if necessary, and ask for spiritual direction from a Catholic you know and trust, who could be a priest, a Religious brother or sister, or a lay-person whom you know to have a firm spiritual foundation. And never forget that the Lord is always there, and that if He wishes you to bear this cross, it will ultimately bring you great good and consolation.

No-one who is suffering, however great or small their cross may be, ever has to suffer alone. Besides the ever-present love of the Trinity and the help of Our Lady and the saints, we may also join with others in pain, men and women who are bravely bearing their own individual cross, and offer one another much-needed companionship in our pilgrimage.

The Catholic organization CUSA (Catholic Union of the Sick in America) is, despite its somewhat misleading name, a world-wide organisation that aims to unite Catholics in many parts of the world so that they may support one another in just this way. We mainly correspond by email, and it keeps us in touch with other members and with our CUSA spiritual director, all of which is a huge help when we need advice or simply a bit of extra encouragement.

Other organisations which offer companionship and practical

help vary according to diocese and country. It would be worthwhile finding out what groups may be available in your locality, not necessarily Catholic, but aimed at helping people like us who may be housebound, or lonely, or just looking for some support. I'm thinking now of – for example – local associations for disabled people, which can be a good place to find others in a similar situation; and groups which provide social contact and sometimes practical help for older people, such as (in the UK) the University of the 3rd Age, and AgeUK.

No doubt there are many more, and during easier times you may want to explore just what sort of help you can access in your area. Since Covid-19 and its lockdowns began, many people world-wide have realised how debilitating loneliness can be, and have come up with new ways to offer support. When you are feeling unwell or in pain you may not be able to exert the effort to find out about them. This is why, once again, it's a good idea to explore your options during easier times, and then you will have the information you need at your fingertips, when you need it.

As well as simple human companionship – a vital component of our lives, whether ill or well, suffering or pain-free – we can all look to the saints for spiritual companionship.

As Catholics, we believe in the Communion of Saints. We know that the saints are as keen to help us as we are to help those in need around us. The saints offer themselves to us as guides through the paths of pain and suffering, because they have all trodden it before us, and know how to persevere to the end. They will hear our prayers for help and are ready to inspire us through their writings, their examples, and their intercession for us with the Lord, from Whom all healing ultimately comes.

We may know them through books, through records of conversations they had with their contemporaries, and through studying their lives. Sometimes they will send us inspirations and intuitions that will prove enormously helpful. During the writing of this book, I've felt inspired and guided by St Therese, among others, not only by reading her autobiography and letters, but also simply through intuitions that I believe she has sent me, prompting me to read such-and-such a page, or turn to a particular source when I needed it.

The saints are alive, like us, but living in the supernatural realm. They are happy to help us, indeed they long to do so!

To conclude this book, therefore, I would like to offer you the example of two more saints, both closer to our time than St. Therese, and both well known for their great courage and perseverance in the face of suffering. Both are Polish, and testify to the enduring power of the church even when demonised by Communism: both were "experts" in suffering with patience, and in offering everything to Christ in union with His own sacred Passion.

Firstly, you may find inspiration in the writings and personal example of that great Holy Father, St John Paul II.

To me, he is one of the strongest witnesses to the power of redemptive suffering that I have ever seen.

From his youth and middle age, when he was a strong, healthy man with tremendous energy and charisma, to his old age, when he was suffering from Parkinson's Disease, he never ceased to minister to the church in every way he could.

At a young age he entrusted himself and his church ministry to Our Lady, and when he become Pope he commended her to all Catholics – indeed, to all Christians – and encouraged everyone to pray the Rosary and offer up their daily lives to Jesus through Mary.

His devotion was rewarded in a miraculous way when, in an assassination attempt, a bullet pierced his chest. He said later that "One hand fired the bullet, another guided it". It was Our Lady, he said, who diverted the bullet from what would have been a fatal trajectory and saved his life. In thanksgiving to her,

St John Paul II made a pilgrimage to Fatima and placed the bullet in Mary's crown, before a huge crowd.

That Mary intervened is clear from many synchronicities. The assassination attempt was made on May 13, 1981, the anniversary of her apparitions to the three children at Fatima. The Pope was rushed to hospital, losing six pints of blood from five different intestinal wounds, and surgeons confirmed that if the bullet had hit the main artery, just a hair's breadth from one of the wounds, death would have been instantaneous.

On the way to hospital, St John Paul II constantly prayed to Mary, and after his recovery he consecrated the whole world to her Immaculate Heart. Following the examples of Jesus and Mary, he even visited the would-be assassin in prison and forgave him. He refused to let the physical suffering he endured harden his heart or interfere with the compassion he felt for all souls, even that of the man who had been paid to kill him.

Many people afflicted with pain become bitter and resentful. They question God's goodness, and may even lose their faith, because their idea of God was limited to that of a heavenly Santa Claus, bringing only pleasant and happy events into their lives. Yet, as we have seen, God permits us to suffer because he knows that ultimately good may result from what we have endured. Part of the great good that came from St John Paul II's assassination attempt was the wonderful example he gave to the world of how we must forgive our enemies and try to do good to them, as Jesus taught.

Another legacy was the strengthening of the faith of millions of Catholics all over the world, who saw how patiently and stoically suffering could be borne. This aspect of the saint's life increased dramatically as he grew older.

Complications from the assassination attempt included infection and the permanent damage to his health that ensued. He was never to regain the great strength and vigour that he had enjoyed until then. Ageing brought an intestinal tumour, an appendectomy, and several falls, one of which resulted in a broken femur.

He was in constant pain from arthritis, an affliction which many of us share.

It was the Parkinson's Disease that was the most visible of his sufferings, however. Slowly it deprived this great saint of the power of movement and even of speech. His last public appearances, in a wheelchair and barely able to speak, testified to his endurance, his courage and his humility. A vain or less brave person would have hidden himself away, but Saint John Paul II would not allow that to happen. He knew his sufferings had a purpose, and he wanted at least one of those purposes to be seen – that of affirming the value, the preciousness, of all life.

For it was then, one prelate said, that the Pope wrote the most beautiful encyclical of his life – it was that which he wrote with his own flesh and blood, in front of the world. It was the value of life itself, of the dignity of the person who is incapacitated and in pain, and reliant on others for basic necessities of life. Even then, reduced in the eyes of some to an inconvenient, even embarrassing, invalid, even then, life is infinitely precious.

In his final years, Saint John Paul II gave the world the lesson we must all one day learn: how to die.

He became in fact a living embodiment of the Suffering Lord, Christ Himself.

No doubt his continued appearances were both painful and damaging to his body. By refusing to retire from public life, the Pope showed how much he loved the Church and the people, and above all how much he loved God.

The world eventually recognised that this man was a great saint. At his funeral there were many calls to make him saint quickly - "Santo Subito!" the crowd shouted – and it was not before he was officially canonised. He has left us the record of his thought, in the encyclicals, books and poems he wrote, and of his endurance of extreme infirmity in the public appearances he made right up until the end of his life.

He wrote that, if the suffering person refuses to give in to fear and perseveres in the difficult way he is called to bear his cross, he will come eventually to the realisation that "suffering will not get the better of him – it will not deprive him of his dignity as a human being, dignity linked to the awareness of the meaning of life".

Moreover, he said, "Each human being is called to share in that suffering through which all human suffering has been redeemed" and that each person, "in his suffering, can become a sharer in the redemptive suffering of Christ".

This great contemporary saint is a remarkable example and guide for each one of us who suffers, whether physically or mentally. We can be sure that if we pray to him for the gift of perseverance, our prayers will be answered.

The second saint is a young woman whose own courage and perseverance inspired St John Paul II. Through her, the world received the message of Divine Mercy, a gift from Jesus which has consoled millions of suffering and sick people all over the world, and inspired millions more to trust in the mercy of God even when everything around them seems hopeless.

She is, of course, St Faustina. Like St Therese, she died young of tuberculosis, and did not live to see the world-wide success of the Divine Mercy message. Her life spanned only 33 years, from 1905 to 1938, yet in that short time she overcame tremendous obstacles to bring the Divine Mercy consolation to the world. Her Diary, together with the Divine Mercy image that Jesus asked her to present, has inspired men and women from every corner of the world to place their trust in Jesus, and to remain hopeful that His mercy will prevail, even in the face of every obstacle.

St Faustina was born to a poor family, and when she became aware of her vocation had to face opposition from her family as well as the need to take on menial work in order to bring a dowry to the convent which accepted her, the Congregation of the Sisters of Our Lady of Mercy, in Warsaw.

She was moved around among a number of different houses belonging to the order, and everywhere was allotted menial tasks similar to those she had carried out before her entry – housework, cookery, gardening and so on. From the time she entered the convent she was criticised and humiliated by the sisters, at first because they deemed her work inadequate, not realising that she was often exhausted and racked with pain, and later because she disclosed the revelations that Jesus had begun to give her.

Eventually, overcoming great opposition, she managed to achieve what the Lord has asked her to do: to give the world a portrait of Jesus which showed two rays emanating from his heart – one red, and one white. The red ray symbolises His blood, and the white ray the water which gushed forth from His side when a Roman soldier pierced His skin with a lance to confirm His death.

Jesus told St Faustina that the water was that which makes souls righteous, and the blood is the life of souls. Together, they symbolise the great mercy which He offers all who turn to Him. At the bottom of the picture are the words that Jesus requested to be written there: "Jesus, I trust in you".

The Lord explained to St Faustina that His heart burned with love for souls, and He wished to pour out His love and mercy upon all who turned to Him. To have confidence in His mercy and to trust in Him were to become increasingly important as the 20th century drew on, and the Second World War broke out and engulfed much of Europe, including the area of Poland where St Faustina had lived.

Even more compelling in our time is the need for trust in

God, when so much of the modern world is under the spell of Satan, and the Church and the family are under attack as never before.

For those of us who are suffering, the message of mercy and trust brings consolation in the darkest times. We are not to despair, whether of our personal well-being or of the fate of the world, for all are in His care, no matter how difficult our lives may become. He will bring good from suffering, when we unite our own personal pain to that which He endured in His Passion.

In persevering to bring Jesus's message to the world, St Faustina was greatly encouraged by St Therese of Lisieux.

She writes in her Diary of a very important dream she had, in which St Therese appeared to her. She says that even before she entered the convent, she had had a great devotion to St Therese, although she had neglected this devotion to some extent. But after the dream, St Faustina again began to pray to St Therese "with great fervour", and she says that St Therese assured her that one day she, too, would be a saint.

St Therese added that, for this to happen, "You must trust in the Lord Jesus." This encouragement helped St Faustina to continue her efforts even when suffering greatly from the resistance she experienced from her sisters and superiors.

Trust, of course, is the theme of the Divine Mercy devotion, and it became a very important part of St John Paul II's spiritual life. He said that, in his view, by giving the world the Divine Mercy image and devotion, Christ had entered our time in a very special way.

So much importance did the Pope give to this message that in 2000, he officially proclaimed her as one of the saints of the Church.

The feast of the Divine Mercy is now held on the first Sunday after Easter, and the image which Jesus gave the world is to be found in virtually every church in every nation of the world, as well as in many homes.

It was St John Paul II's death in 2005 that saw the stories of the two saints become forever intertwined, for the Pope died on the eve of that very feast day, just after he had received the Eucharist in the form of the Precious Blood, during the Vigil Mass for Divine Mercy Sunday.

Before his death that evening, St John Paul II had already written the sermon he wanted to be read out on Divine Mercy Sunday. It emphasized the fact that trust in Jesus was the most urgent need for the individual and the world in our time.

"How much the world needs to understand and accept Divine Mercy", he had written. The sermon continued, "Jesus, I trust in you: have mercy on us and the whole world". The last sentence repeats the words of the Chaplet of Divine Mercy, which is an important part of that devotion.

It is a message that we who suffer, and who can sometimes be tempted to despair, very much need to keep in our awareness today.

That it was brought into the world by two saints who knew, from the inside, what it was to suffer agonisingly and yet never yielded to despair, can encourage us to renew our own hope and trust in the Lord.

That its birth was also partly due to the encouragement of St Therese, the saint whose example we have studied throughout this book, shows us how closely these great saints are connected in their devotion to the love and mercy of Jesus.

I will end with a quotation from St John Paul II, on the role of suffering in the life of the Christian.

"Those who share in the sufferings of Christ preserve in their own sufferings a very special particle of the infinite treasure of the world's Redemption, and can share this treasure with others," he wrote.

Note the last part of that quotation: we may not only join our sufferings to those of the Crucified Christ, we may also share this treasure with others. How? By performing works of mercy ourselves.

Perhaps we cannot go out and visit the sick, or minister to the dying, but wherever we may be, we can offer our sufferings in prayer to Jesus, and ask Him to use them for good in His work of Redemption.

That is the priceless gift of suffering that He gives us. That is how we may turn our sufferings into joy, thanks to His great mercy.

What a glorious act we perform, when we turn everything over to Him, and trust in His mercy.

It is my heartfelt wish that all who suffer, in whatever way, may find this precious way of transforming pain and sorrow into joy.

May God help you to find your peace and joy in serving Him through your very weakness, as He has done for me and for so many others throughout the ages.

Appendix I

A note on Dr Maurice Nicoll and The Work

Dr Maurice Nicoll was a noted Harley Street psychiatrist who had studied with Carl Jung before opening his own private practice.

Dr Nicoll had also studied the system of psychological and spiritual transformation that became known as The Work, or The Fourth Way. This system was thoroughly Christian in its ideas and applications. It originated in Russia with the teachings of George Gurdjieff and Pyotr Ouspensky, but quickly spread to Europe and America. It now has study groups all over the world.

Gurdjieff, who was the first to teach The Work, said that its aim was to teach people how to be Christian.

"It is the ABC of Christianity," he explained. He went on to say that if you can behave like a Christian only after you have had your morning coffee, you were not really Christian at all!

Dr Nicoll taught The Work to small groups in England and went on to write the most clear and thorough account of its psychological applications in a five-volume work, "Psychological Commentaries on the Teachings of G. I. Gurdjieff and P. D. Ouspensky".

He stated, "The Work is the inner meaning of Christ's sayings and parables, and (this) is what the Work teaches."

As well as the Commentaries, Dr Nicoll also wrote two books on the Gospels and a discussion on the nature of time.

See the Bibliography at the end of this book for details.

Appendix II: Christian Contemplation

Christian contemplation is very simple to do, and regular practice will allow you to experience the love and peace which the Holy Spirit bestows on each soul which is in a state of grace, and wishes to draw closer to God.

It is not absolutely essential for your well being or your spiritual growth, but in my experience I have found it greatly helps with both. To set aside a period of time each day to simply exist under the gaze of God, and to be filled with His peace and His compassion, has transformed my understanding and experience of His Presence.

There are a number of ways to practise Christian contemplation, but this is the method I regularly use.

First, choose a time which is convenient for you and which you can make a convenient daily rendezvous for your meeting with God.

Usually, for me, the time just after breakfast is what works best, and generally it is good to start the day in this way. Some people also set aside a second period, just before dinner, but in my own life I haven't found this either possible or necessary.

Whatever time you have chosen, seek out a place where you will not be interrupted for at least 20 minutes.

Sit quietly and comfortably in your chair, close your eyes, and choose a word which will remind you of God's Presence and His love. Many people, myself included, choose the name of Jesus. Others have suggested the phrase "Ave Maria", or the words "Peace", "Mercy", "Love", "Bless", or – as one well-known teacher uses - a word from scripture, "Maranatha", which means, "Come, Lord".

Begin repeating your chosen word silently. Allow your word

to become the focus of your attention, so that other thoughts and images fall away. After a while, if you realise you have forgotten your word, simply return to it and begin again.

After your period of contemplation draws to a close, pray the Lord's Prayer, and slowly and gently return to your surroundings.

Regular practice brings greater peace and serenity to your daily life, and that precious morning prayer time becomes a force for stability that allows you to deepen your relationship with God.

As for the length of time you should stay in contemplation, this will depend partly on your schedule. For beginners, ten minutes may be all you can manage for the first week or so. Eventually you will want to extend it, and for me and many others around 20 minutes to half an hour is the optimal period of time for this practice.

It is fine to open your eyes in order to check the time, but after a while you will probably find you no longer need to do this – your mind will tell you when it's time to return to your surroundings and end the meditation.

For more information, the books of Father Thomas Keating and Father Basil Pennington have proved extremely helpful to many.

See the Bibliography at the end of this book.

Bibliography

Life and teachings of St Therese of Lisieux:-
St Therese – Story of a Soul – Tan Books, 2010
The Hidden Face – Ida Gorres, Ignatius Press, 2003
Everything is Grace – Joseph Schmidt, Word Among Us Press, 2007

The Writings of Maurice Nicoll:-
The New Man: An Interpretation of Some Parables – Martino Press, 2019
Psychological Commentaries on the Teachings of Gurdjieff and Ouspensky –
Vols 1-5 – Shambhala Publications, 1984

Christian Meditation:-
Centering Prayer – Father Basil Pennington, Image, 2010
Open Mind, Open Heart – Father Thomas Keating, Bloomsbury Continuum, 2019
Intimacy With God – Father Thomas Keating, Crossroads Publishing, 2009

Suffering:-
Healing – You and Your Family Tree – Father Christopher Ngozi Onuaha, Independently Published, 2022
The Mystery of Suffering – Hubert Van Zeller, Ave Maria Press, 2015
The Pain That Heals – Martin Israel, Mowbray, 1983
The Light Shines on in the Darkness – Father Robert Spitzer, Ignatius Press, 2017

About the Author

Dr Elizabeth Stewart was born in 1944 in England. In 1983, while living in Atlanta, Georgia, she suffered a major traffic accident in which most of her bones, from pelvis to feet, were shattered, her gluteal and sciatic nerves were damaged, and one lung was punctured. She spent several months in hospital while her bones were rebuilt as far as possible. During this time she read the autobiography of St Therese of Lisieux and by the grace of God became converted to the Catholic faith. Dr Stewart has two adult daughters, and she and her husband now live in England.